MELLIN DE SAINT-GELAIS
AND
LITERARY HISTORY

DONALD STONE, JR.

FRENCH FORUM, PUBLISHERS
LEXINGTON, KENTUCKY

Library of Congress Catalog Card Number 83-81183

ISBN 0-917058-47-X

Printed in the United States of America

For Gwyneth and Sheila

PREFACE

It is only by chance that the completion of this manuscript corresponds to the preparation for Oxford University Press of a volume of essays on neo-Latin poetry and to the planning at the University of New Orleans of an international symposium on pre-Pléiade poetry. Nevertheless, it is hoped that the coincidence will prove a happy one, with each effort complementing the perspective of the others and emphasizing anew the importance of the literature written just before publication of the *Deffence*.

Since my study is based in part upon a number of texts from that period which can be found only in rare-book libraries, the most essential of these texts have been appended to the appropriate chapter so that they may reach the public they deserve.

Over the years that this monograph has been in preparation, many individuals have generously given their time, advice and support. I wish to thank in particular the librarians of the Bibliothèque Nationale (Salle de Réserve) and the Musée Condé, Richard Thomas of the Harvard Classics Department, as well as the Harvard Graduate Society, which permitted me to visit the European libraries one final time. Grahame Castor and Terence Cave, who read earlier versions of the manuscript and spoke their piece forthrightly, I must single out for special thanks not only because my debt to their wisdom is considerable, but also because the profession should know of the extent of their generosity. In a similar way, although the individuals to whom this work is dedicated will, I am confident, understand my intent, it is high time that others hear of my gratitude for their abiding friendship.

Cambridge, Mass.
Summer 1982

Abbreviations used in the text, notes and bibliography

BHR   *Bibliothèque d'Humanisme et Renaissance*
MLN   *Modern Language Notes*
RHLF   *Revue d'Histoire Littéraire de la France*
RSH   *Revue des Sciences Humaines*
RSS   *Revue du Seizième Siècle*

References to the psalms

Given that a difference exists between the Catholic and Protestant tradition with regard to the numbering of the psalms, an evident problem arises when reference to those songs is called for. Because of the importance of Marot's translations for the period under investigation, the text to follow adopts throughout the numbering used by Marot, generally one figure higher than the sequence found in the Vulgate.

CONTENTS

Chapter I

THE ISSUES

Now that time has firmly established the worth of the Pléiade, it may not seem important that many pages in the *Deffence et illustration de la langue françoyse* are derived from the arguments of earlier writers or that in 1549 the work advanced ideas which were not new to the world of French literature. For those who would equate the Pléiade poets with their undeniable talent and innumerable poetic triumphs, these facts of literary history must pale before the worth of their writings.

By the same token, such respect for the Pléiade's accomplishments gives continued impetus to study of the *Deffence*, if only because it contains hints of the greatness to come. No admirer of the Pléiade can fail to exult in the finality with which Du Bellay discards the past: "Ly donques & rely . . . les exemplaires Grecz & Latins: puis me laisse toutes ces vieilles poësies Francoyses aux Jeuz Floraux de Thoulouze & au Puy de Rouan: comme rondeaux, ballades, vyrelaiz, chantz royaulx, chansons, & autres telles episseries, qui corrumpent le goust de nostre Langue" (ed. Chamard, pp. 107-08),[1] or in the way he proceeds to call for the replacement of these forms with such possibilities as the sonnet and the ode, genres which over the years have provided the vehicle for countless masterpieces of French literature. The danger, of course, is that, while exulting in these outbursts of a new esthetic sense, we may forget that the *Deffence* is a polemical document, one that cannot be confused with objective literary history, however straightforward its statements on the literature of the day may appear, and that, as a result, recognizing the polemical nature of the *Deffence* obliges us to put those statements to the test.

For example. the passages from the *Deffence* just quoted can be found in Book II, chapter iv, which, with its list of genres so roundly rejected by Du Bellay, suggests that the ballade, rondeau, chant royal and virelai enjoyed great favor in the 1540s. Yet nothing is less true.

The years 1540-1548 produced a number of volumes of new verse:

1540   Charles de Sainte-Marthe, *La Poésie françoise de Charles de Sainte-Marthe*
1542   Le Seigneur de La Borderie, *Le Discours du voyage de Constantinople*
1544   Bonaventure Des Périers, *Recueil des œuvres de feu Bonaventure Des Périers*
        Maurice Scève, *Délie*
1545   Antoine Du Moulin, *Déploration de Vénus sur la mort du bel Adonis*
        Charles Fontaine, *La Fontaine d'amour*
        Pernette du Guillet, *Rymes*
1547   Mellin de Saint-Gelais, *Saingelais, Oeuvres de luy tant en composition, que translation*
        Jacques Peletier du Mans, *Les Oeuvres poétiques*
        Marguerite de Navarre, *Les Marguerites de la Marguerite des princesses*
1548   Etienne Forcadel, *Le Chant des seraines*

Significantly, the only *recueil* to contain an appreciable quantity of rondeaux, ballades and chants royaux is the earliest, Sainte-Marthe's *Poésie françoise* (pp. 81-112). Many (the works of Scève, Du Moulin, Fontaine, La Borderie, Pernette and Peletier du Mans) offer no example of these genres at all. The remainder (Des Périers, Saint-Gelais, Marguerite and Forcadel) contain only a meager amount of medieval *formes fixes*,[2] especially if we note in what numbers other genres are represented. Des Périers's *Recueil* presents 34 epigrams to six rondeaux and one ballade; Saint-Gelais's *Oeuvres*, 38 epigrams to two rondeaux, no ballades and no virelais. This preponderance of epigrams can be observed throughout the period. The first book of Sainte-Marthe's *Poésie françoise* is devoted to epigrams (pp. 7-80); Scève's *Délie*, of course, contains only epigrams. Pernette's *Rymes* reveal 54 epigrams to ten chansons and five elegies. Fontaine's *La Fontaine d'amour* is divided among, on the one hand, 97 epigrams (followed by *Deux Livres d'épigrammes du mesme autheur*) and, on the other hand, 22 elegies and nineteen épîtres (the two genres reserved for the third book in Sainte-Marthe's volume, pp. 113-224).

Thus, despite the nature of Du Bellay's reference to the rondeau, ballade, chant royal and virelai, the years immediately preceding publication of the *Deffence* give proof rather of a preponderance of epigrams, elegies and épîtres, and, to a lesser degree, of chansons (the dominant genre in Du Moulin's *Déploration* and *Les Marguerites*).[3] Did Du Bellay distort these facts because of his wish to counter the thrust of Sébillet's *Art poétique* of 1548, a work that gives serious attention to the genres Du Bellay dismisses as "episseries"? If so, again the polemics of the *Deffence* mislead, since Sébillet presents the censured genres in a light fully consonant with historical reality.

In the *Art poétique*, the parade of genres begins with the epigram, followed by the sonnet, since, according to Sébillet, "Sonnet n'est autre chose que le parfait epigramme de l'Italien, comme le dizain du François" (ed. Gaiffe, p. 115). As if this prominence awarded the epigram and sonnet were not surprising enough, when (with the third chapter) we arrive at his discussion of the rondeau, it is to learn that this form no longer enjoys the esteem it once had, "Car pource que la matiére du Rondeau n'est autre que du sonnet ou épigramme, lés Pöétes de ce temps lés plus frians ont quitté lés Rondeaus a l'antiquité [read: Middle Ages], pour s'arrester aus Epigrammes et Sonnetz, Pöémes de premier pris entre lés petis. Et de fait tu lis peu de Rondeaus de Saingelais, Sceve, Salel, Héröet . . ." (ed. Gaiffe, p. 120). The opening lines of Chapter XIII ("Du Lay et Virelay") prove to be even more negative: "Je te pensoie avoir touché toutes lés différences et espéces de poémes, quant m'est souvenu du Lay et Virelay: lesquelz, pour le peu d'usage qu'ilz ont aujourd'huy entre lés Pöétes celebrés, j'eusse aisement laissé a te declarer, si je n'eusse creint faire tort a l'antiquité" (ed. Gaiffe, p. 180).

Would we ever have divined this from the *Deffence*? I think not. To encounter the attitude Du Bellay denounces, we have to move farther back in time to a work such as Pierre Fabri's *Le grant et vray art de pleine rhétorique*, first printed in 1521, or to Gracien Du Pont's *Art et science de rhétorique métriffiée* (Toulouse, 1539), a treatise strongly influenced by Fabri. The second book of Fabri's treatise, entitled "L'Art de rithmer," proceeds from a discussion of rhyme schemes and verse length to consideration of what we might call today "genres," although Fabri does not use the word. The forms—rhythme de deux et ar, lay, virelay, rondeaux, bergerette, pastourelle, chapelets, pallinode, epilogue, reffrain branlant, ballade, septains, chanson, champ royal and servantoys—as defined by Fabri exist at varying degrees of independence from each other, and the number of examples provided, as well as the relative space assigned to each form, suffices to indicate that the pivotal patterns correspond to those genres Du Bellay labeled "episseries."

The treatise was reprinted in 1534, 1536, 1539 and 1544, a strong suggestion that its contents did not lose their appeal, despite the lack of interest that is exhibited in the short, epigrammatic forms. (Telling in this regard is Fabri's inclusion of the septain, which the theoretician discusses in relation not to the huitain or the dizain, but to the ballade: "Septains different a ballade, pource qu'ilz sont de sept lignes, et ballade est de huyt, et la septiesme de septains en lieu de reffrain doibt estre vne auctorité ou vng prouerbe commun . . . ," ed. Héron, II, 91.)

Although Du Pont's treatise of 1539 perpetuates many retrograde traits of *Le grant et vray art de pleine rhétorique* (review of the old *formes fixes*, indifference to the word "épigramme" and what it came to designate, equation of the septain with the ballade), what aspiring poets studied does not necessarily equal what they were producing. "Les Fleurs de poésie françoyse," an anthology of verse accompanying a French translation of Alberti's *Hecatomphilia* printed in Paris in 1534, contains 64 poems. Of these, only one bears the title "Chant royal." Four are rondeaux, whereas 47 are epigrams. The proportions speak for themselves. Even before 1540 the epigram had attained a distinct importance. After that date, its prominence is assured. Sébillet implies this, and the evidence of the *recueils* published in the decade confirms it.

How, we might well ask, have we failed to stress adequately both the degree of polemical misrepresentation by the *Deffence* and the historical reality misrepresented? Barthélemy Aneau may have to shoulder part of the blame. The stance he adopts when reacting to the *Deffence* in his *Quintil Horatian* so often reinforces our sense of Du Bellay's annoyance with the poetry of the day that we readily believe that Du Bellay is fighting the good fight.

Aneau's response can be now self-serving (his charge that Du Bellay rejected the medieval *formes fixes* because he could not master their difficulty), now unfortunate (his claim that what is difficult is also beautiful). The mentality behind the second remark resurfaces when Aneau attacks Du Bellay's preference for the sonnet over the older forms. For him, the sonnet is no more than a huitain followed by a sizain, but a sizain in which, contrary to French practices with the six-line form, the rhymes are arranged "abandonnéement & deregléement" (cited in Chamard's ed. of the *Deffence*, p. 120). Here Aneau is confirming a long-standing conviction of literary historians that the works of the Rhétoriqueurs contain mere verbal acrobatics and fascination with complex forms. Thus, as the *Quintil Horatian* unfolds, Aneau seems to justify both Du Bellay's protests against a dismal native tradition in French letters and any modern hesitation to take too seriously contemporary opposition to the *Deffence*.

Just as our preoccupation with the *Deffence* has brought us to devalue the *Quintil Horatian*, so it has allowed us to pass over another statement about French verse in the 1540s penned by a Renaissance writer. Instructive indeed, however, is this remark by Etienne Pasquier, who was Ronsard's junior by only five years. Speaking of developments in poetry during the reign of Henry II, he writes: "Ce fut vne belle guerre que l'on entreprit lors contre l'ignorance" (p. 616). After reading the *Deffence*, we would presume that Pasquier is referring to the efforts of Du Bellay and Ronsard, but our assumption would be only partially correct. Here is the full passage: "Ce fut vne belle guerre que l'on entreprit lors contre l'ignorance, dont j'attribuë l'auant-garde à Seue, Beze, & Pelletier, ou si le voulez autrement, ce furent les auant-coureurs des autres Poëtes. Apres se mirent sur les rangs, Pierre de Ronsard Vandomois, & Ioachim du Bellay Angeuin . . ." (*Recherches*, pp. 616-17).

The schema sketched by Pasquier is clear enough. Certain poets already published before Du Bellay composed the *Deffence* are seen as preparing the way for the Pléiade. The three names designated as "auant-coureurs," to wit, Scève, Bèze and Peletier, have long figured in literary histories of the period, but not always in this role. Only Peletier occupies in such histories the place accorded him by Pasquier. Scève's use of emblems and the dizain form alone serves to distinguish him from the love cycles produced by the Pléiade, whose judgment on the poet appears to have been somewhat ambivalent. Admiring, when citing Scève by name, the Pléiade also made unflattering references to the verse of an obscure poet, generally assumed to be Scève (e.g., Du Bellay in the *Deffence*, p. 96, and Baïf in the last poem of the first book of *Les Amours de Méline*). Bèze's name must be the most unexpected. His first book contained poems in Latin—the *Poemata* of 1548—and we are so accustomed to equating the *Deffence* with a crucial blow for the pre-eminence of French over Latin that not only the name of Bèze, but also his early writings seem incompatible with Pasquier's text. Yet that text is unambiguous.

The text is also somewhat helpful with regard to pinpointing the source of Pasquier's admiration. "Ceux-cy du commencement," he writes, "firent profession de plus contenter leurs esprits que l'opinion du commun peuple" (p. 615). The passage implies that these individuals broke with a tendency to write pleasing, but traditional and plebeian verse, a conclusion that is partially supported by Pasquier's choice of words to describe the three poets. He singles out for comment Scève's *Délie* ("à l'imitation des Italiens"), Peletier's dialogue on the reform of French orthography, Bèze's translations from the psalms and *Abraham Sacrifiant* ("bien retiré [tracé] au vif"). If we read into the list a preoccupation with reform, innovation and excellence, its presence within Pasquier's discussion of a "war against ignorance" makes perfect sense. Yet it is also curious, regarding these "auant-coureurs," to find now reference to two works that postdate publication of the *Deffence* and *L'Olive—Abraham Sacrifiant* (1550) and Peletier's *Dialogue* (1550)—now a lack of concern for such impressive facts as Bèze's use of Greek tragedy for his play or Peletier's incorporation in the *Oeuvres poétiques* of 1548 of translations from Petrarch and Horace. The possibility cannot be overlooked, therefore, that this list was not meant to be a precise illustration of Pasquier's point concerning those who "firent profession . . . de contenter leurs esprits," but only a general allusion to their accomplishments.[4]

The absence of more specific information as to Pasquier's reasons for giving prominence to Scève, Bèze and Peletier can prove off-putting. All three poets participated extensively in the fascination with the epigram exhibited throughout the 1540s. The dizain form used by Scève in *Délie* represents, according to Sébillet, the perfect epigrammatic vehicle in French; Bèze's *Poemata* contains no fewer than 98 epigrams. Peletier's *Oeuvres poétiques* offers seventeen works under the rubric of the epigram, including a blason and a contreblason and poems inspired by the Queen, Marguerite de Valois, Cardinal Du Bellay, and Francis I. Yet Scève, Bèze and Peletier emerge from the *Recherches* as both soldiers in a war against ignorance and as "auant-coureurs des autres Poëtes." By "Poëtes" Pasquier clearly means the Pléiade, even though the Pléiade cannot be said to have favored the epigram. Baïf's epigrams are relegated to the obviously secondary category of *Les Passetems*, and even those which Pontus de Tyard published in his *Erreurs amoureuses* in 1549, that is, at a time when the genre still mattered, are sprinkled among the far more numerous sonnets. The reasons that brought Pasquier to make his pronouncement cannot, it would seem, be easily discerned. However, as the pages to follow will attempt to show, research into the decade preceding the *Deffence* reveals the existence of sufficient literary activity to justify certain remarks in *Les Recherches de la France* which do point in interesting directions.

For example, Pasquier has praise for Bèze's psalms, but even more praise for the translations of the same sacred texts produced by Marot. These translations call to mind the fact that the attention once accorded the epigram was given by the Pléiade to the sonnet and to the ode, a strophic form in the mold of Marot's rendering of the biblical songs. Is there some reason to suppose that Marot's translations and general interest in the psalms contribute to preparing a new lyric form? The *Deffence* discourages such a supposition. By establishing a stark contrast between the medieval *formes fixes* and its preferred genres, the Pléiade implies for the future of French letters a schema of rupture, of inherited genres discarded and foreign genres adapted to the native lyre. But here the polemics of the *Deffence* are unmistakable.

Consider instead the work of Paul Laumonier, whose *Ronsard poète lyrique* remains our surest guide to the background of pre-Pléiade lyric poetry. There Laumonier reminds us that Fabri recognized in his treatise to what degree the ballade and chant royal were undergoing changes in structure that in effet signal movement among the medieval *formes fixes* towards the newer lyric modes (p. 643). It is my belief that experimentation with lyric poetry continued uninterrupted throughout the 1540s, quite in the midst of the burgeoning of the epigram, well in advance of the publication of *Abraham Sacrifiant* and Peletier's *Dialogue*, and along lines fully consistent with the clearest statement from the *Recherches* characterizing the so-called "fore-runners," that is, their desire "de plus contenter leurs esprits que l'opinion du commun peuple."

At the center of our investigation stands Mellin de Saint-Gelais (1491-1558). Officially the nephew, but more likely the son, of Octavian de Saint-Gelais, Mellin held the prestigious post of aumônier to Henry II, participating all the while in and writing poetry for the social life of the French court. His works were well received, and only Marot enjoyed greater success in the years preceding the advent of the Pléiade. Unlike Marot, however, whose innovative spirit C.A. Mayer underscores many times when introducing the various volumes of his critical edition of the poet's works, or unlike other successful poets of the 1540s such as Charles Fontaine or Charles de Sainte-Marthe, in whom scholars have espied links to the Pléiade,[5] Saint-Gelais is still best known as an opponent of the new school. Much has been made of Mellin's apparent criticism of Ronsard's Pindaric odes and of his lack of concern over publication of his poems. In the words of the lone scholar to have devoted an entire book to Saint-Gelais, "Tout entier adonné aux plaisirs de la Cour, il n'avait recherché que le succès du moment" (Molinier, p. 319).

The distance between Mellin and the Pléiade can be charted by actions and attitudes on the side of the Coqueret poets as well. In truth, the first blow in the confrontation was struck by Du Bellay, who, as we shall soon see, excoriated two of Mellin's lyric poems in a passage from the *Deffence*. We begin with Du Bellay's remarks on Mellin's two works in order to assess more fully his statement with respect not only to the text of Saint-Gelais's poems, but later, in Chapter II, with respect also to facets of literary history towards which Saint-Gelais's poems direct our attention. Finally, Mellin and the Pléiade are examined further in a context of special import to the "war against ignorance": the use of Italian and classical models. In each instance, it is hoped, the reader will discover new and useful information about Saint-Gelais and the literary history of which the poet proves to be so intriguing a part.

Chapter II

THE *DEFFENCE* SPEAKS

1. "Laissez la verde couleur"

In Book II, chapter iv of the *Deffence*, nowhere is Du Bellay's attack against his contemporaries—especially Thomas Sébillet and Saint-Gelais—more pointed than in his remarks on the ode. Under the heading of "Du Cantique, Chant Lyrique ou Ode et Chanson," Sébillet's *Art poétique* of 1548 had singled out as a suitable model for lyric expression Saint-Gelais, "qui en est Autheur tant dous que divin: comme tu pourras juger lisant ceste Ode sienne faite au nom d'une Damoiselle" (ed. Gaiffe, p. 148). The poem then quoted in its entirety is Saint-Gelais's "O combien est heureuse." Du Bellay's reaction is categorical: "Sur toutes choses prens garde que ce genre de poëme [the ode] soit eloingné du vulgaire, enrichy & illustré de motz propres & epithetes non oysifz, . . . non comme un *Laissez la verde couleur, Amour avecques Psyches, O combien est heureuse*, & autrez telz ouvraiges, mieux dignes d'estre nommez chansons vulgaires qu'odes ou vers lyriques" (ed. Chamard, pp. 113-15). The desire to correct Sébillet cannot be missed, any more than Du Bellay's dismissal of the writing of his day. All three poems selected for censure were printed for the first time in the 1540s, and both authors in question (Saint-Gelais for "Laissez la verde couleur" and "O combien est heureuse" and Pernette du Guillet for "Amour avecques Psyches") flourished in the decade preceding publication of the *Deffence*.

The immediate context in which Du Bellay lists these three poems would suggest that they had been chosen on the basis of language or style, that is, with respect to those qualities which violate Du Bellay's criteria for the ode. However, the history of the publication of these poems intimates something else.

Only two of the three receive mention in Sébillet's *Art poétique*. As we have noted, "O combien est heureuse" is there reproduced in full; "Laissez la verde couleur" is merely listed among four further examples of Saint-Gelais's "perfection." But both poems had been gathered together by Antoine Du Moulin and printed at the head of an anthology of lyric verse to which Du Moulin gave the general title *Déploration de Vénus sur la mort du bel Adonis, avec plusieurs autres compositions nouvelles* (Lyon, 1545). Beginning with the enlarged edition of *Le Discours du voyage de Constantinople* (Paris, 1546), the three poems censured by Du Bellay appear together, as they do later in the Du Moulin reimpressions of the *Déploration* (Lyon, 1547 and 1548). The works are published a second time in 1548 in a Lyon reprinting of the contents of *Le Discours du voyage de Constantinople*, now entitled *Le Livre de plusieurs pièces*. In every instance the poems follow in the order in which Du Bellay places them in the *Deffence*. "O combien est heureuse" also figures in the 1548 Paris anthology entitled *Chansons nouvellement composées sur plusieurs chants, tant de musique que rustique*. The text has been severely altered, but not enough to cast doubt on the ultimate source of the lines.[1]

Such popularity, further hinted at by the fact that, in the very year that "O combien est heureuse" appeared in print for the first time, Denisot published a noël to be sung to the tune of Saint-Gelais's poem,[2] implies a desire on Du Bellay's part to discredit some of the most successful poetry of the day. This revelation cannot come as a surprise in view of the polemical brashness of the *Deffence*, but it does constitute a useful backdrop against which to explore further facts relating to "Laissez la verde couleur," since the more we learn about the poem the more perplexing Du Bellay's judgment of it becomes.

Like "Amour avecques Psyches," "Laissez la verde couleur" deals with the legend of Adonis, and both poems show the clear imprint of Greek works on that subject, works attributed in the sixteenth century to Theocritus. Did Saint-Gelais consult the Greek sources directly? The fact that the Bibliothèque Nationale possesses a bilingual (Greek/Latin) volume of Stobaeus with the ex libris of our poet only complicates the question, since Saint-Gelais could have wanted the book because the Greek text alone was incomprehensible to him or, on the contrary, because he wished to improve his familiarity with Greek through comparison with the Latin translation. A more promising avenue to explore is provided by Saint-Gelais's epigrams in the manner of the Greek Anthology, even though, despite several references to Greek sources in literature on Saint-Gelais,[3] convincing evidence for direct borrowings must be restricted to relatively few poems.[4] Yet it is substantial enough to posit that Saint-Gelais may have read his two Greek sources on Adonis in the original. In any case, were difficult passages in the Greek encountered, Mellin knew Latin well enough to read the published translations in that language of both poems, one, a Bion idyll ("Adonis' Epitaph"), the other, a work by Pseudo-Theocritus ("Death of Adonis").[5] The Bion text was available, moreover, in Italian adaptations of the Greek by Alamanni and Amomo, and a case can be made for the influence of each on "Laissez la verde couleur."[6] Pernette's "Amour avecques Psyches" does not appear to have any source other than the "Death of Adonis"; however, as is indicated by the poem's title in later editions ("Conde Claros de Adonis"), Pernette was setting her poem to a Spanish air. Saint-Gelais may have intended to do the same. "Laissez la verde couleur" carries in a Bibliothèque Nationale manuscript the title "Lamentation de Venus en la mort d'Adonis, pour reciter en façon de conte clare d'Espagne."

The convergence in "Laissez la verde couleur" of elements from Greek, Spanish and Italian literature (with the possible intervention of Latin) is yet another fact of literary history we would hardly expect from Du Bellay's characterization of the literature of his predecessors. Still, this convergence does not in any way exhaust the provocative facts surrounding Saint-Gelais and "Laissez la verde couleur."

In his *Naeniarum libri tres* (1550), Salmon Macrin included a work entitled "Adonis Theocriti ex Mellini Sangelasii Cantilena."[7] By all rights we should be reading a Latin translation of

"Laissez la verde couleur." In two articles V.-L. Saulnier leads us to believe that such is the case; only near the close of the first article in date does he add: "Mais en réalité, la pièce latine semble se contenter de transporter les vers du pseudo-Thércrite" [sic].[8] And so it does. It reworks the same Greek text that inspired Pernette (although the author most likely composed the "Cantilena" with a 1530 Latin translation of Pseudo-Theocritus close at hand.)[9] As a result, the "Cantilena" overlaps with "Laissez la verde couleur" only in those very few verses that Saint-Gelais, too, borrowed from Pseudo-Theocritus.[10]

This "Cantilena" of 1550 treats the Pseudo-Theocritus poem in a most interesting way. The original Greek work is written in heptasyllabic verse. Both Pernette and the Latin version of 1530 preserve the short line. Not so the "Cantilena." The simple opening "Adoniden Cytharea / Vt uidit interemptum" (sig. L1^v) becomes "Quae Diua Cyprum quaeǫue Paphum tenet / Postquam interemptum uidit Adonidem" (p. 141). Venus' question to the boar,

> Quid pessimạ ò ferarum
> Tu ne hoc femur decorum[,]
> Meum ne tu puellum
> Insana uulnerasti?
>
> (sig. L1^r)

is reworked and expanded upon to read:

> ferarum ô pessima quid (malum?)
> Pulchrum quid inuadens Adonin
> Dente fero modò sauciasti?
> En ille ceu flos uomere ferreo
> Succisus, herba nunc uiridi super
> Pallescit extentus, suoǫue
> Tingit humum roseo cruore.
> Non te mouebat purpureus decor
> Formosi ephebi, non niueum femur,
> Et qui per albentes uolabant
> Auricomi scapulas capilli?
>
> (pp. 142-43)

Finally, "Sed ut decora uidi / Labra & uultus honesti" (sig. L2r)
becomes "Illius ast ut labra coralina / Vultumáque uidi floridulum" (p. 143). Each example tells its own story—now the introduction of erudition and dynamic, even dramatic imagery, now
the injection of more vivid, more specifically poetic vocabulary,
all traits of the new poetry urged by the Pléiade and, in particular, of lyric poetry: "Sur toutes choses, prens garde que ce genre
de poëme soit eloingné du vulgaire, enrichy & illustré de motz
propres & epithetes non oysifz . . . ."

Whoever determined to translate the Greek verses on Adonis
into Latin did more than announce various principles of concern
to the Pléiade. The poet in question also used specific turns of
phrase which, like the literary antecedents for "Laissez la verde
couleur," relate the world of Saint-Gelais to the practice of the
Coqueret poets. The image of the "labra coralina" never appears
in Ovid, Catullus or Virgil, but one Marot epigram begins "Bouche de coral precieux";[11] and in *Délie*, dizain 235, we read of
the lady's "levres corallines." Ronsard uses "coral" and "corail"
no fewer than three times in poems published before the *Amours*
of 1552 and then six times in the *Amours*. In every instance the
words are used as in the "Cantilena," that is, to describe a phys-
ical trait, and five instances relate the word directly to the lips.
Du Bellay uses the image three times in *L'Olive*, and each time
it describes the lady's lips.

As so often happens with Renaissance love poetry, establishing
precise models or sources for the poems containing this image
proves difficult. The various critical editions of Marot, Scève,
Ronsard and Du Bellay send us to fairly predictable antecedents,
all from Italian literature save one. But in truth none of the Italian passages singled out by the poets' editors use the equivalent
of "coral." Indeed, McKenzie's concordance to the *Canzoniere*
assures us that neither "corallo" nor "corallino" ever occurs
in that work and Ariosto prefers "cinabro" when describing
Alcina's mouth in the famous passage from the *Furioso* used by
innumerable Renaissance poets when drawing a portrait of their
beloved. The image was, nonetheless, prevalent in Italian love
poetry of the period. Mellin even repeats it in a poem which cat-
alogues the images characteristic of contemporary Italian and

Spanish love lyrics;[12] Sassoferrato uses it in two successive strambotti and in a frottola printed in 1523 and reprinted in 1544.[13] The image appears also in Second's eighteenth basium (the one non-Italian source proposed for Ronsard's image), and it may not be a coincidence that one appearance of the image of coral lips among the sonnets of *L'Olive* helps to fill out a work in the basia tradition, even though the poem's central conceit has roots in Italian verse:[14]

> Au goust de l'eau la fievre se rappaise,
> Puis s'evertue au cours, qui sembloit lent:
> Amour aussi m'est humble et violent,
> Quand le coral de voz levres je baise.
>
> L'eau goute à goute anime la fournaize
> D'un feu couvert le plus etincelant:
> L'ardent desir, que mon cœur va celant,
> Par voz baisers se faict plus chault que braize.
>
> D'un grand traict d'eau, qui freschement distile,
> Souvent la fievre est etainte, Madame.
> L'onde à grand flot rent la flamme inutile.
>
> Mais, ô baisers, delices de mon ame!
> Vous ne pouriez, et fussiez vous cent mile,
> Guerir ma fievre ou eteindre ma flamme.
>   (XLIV)

Even more intriguing, as we continue to find elements of some continuity between Mellin's world and the Pléiade, is to note that these elements, including Saint-Gelais's name, are all associated with a Latin poem that reproduces Horace's favorite meter: the Alcaic Strophe. Before expressing surprise, however, at this linking of Saint-Gelais with an Horatian form, we might recall that both "Laissez la verde couleur" and "Amour avecques Psyches" were on occasion offered to the century as poems patterned on a Spanish air, that is, as works related to the musical chanson. Our unnamed translator, it would seem, determined to match the lyricism of these two French poems with a lyric mode from one of the great Roman poets.

Such an association could not be farther from the perspective on "Laissez la verde couleur," "Amour avecques Psyches" and

"O combien est heureuse" that Du Bellay expresses in the *Deffence*, but, then, the evidence of the period has already taught us an unexpected lesson about dominant genres in the 1540s. Now additional information points to admiration for Saint-Gelais on the part of a connoisseur of the lyric mode, an imitator of Horace. It may be useful, therefore, to look again at the way in which Du Bellay phrases his dismissal of the three poems cited by title in his manifesto.

2. "Mieux dignes d'estre nommez chansons vulgaires"

The terminology employed by Du Bellay in chapter iv of Book II of the *Deffence* sometimes proves very difficult to interpret. For example, what exactly did Du Bellay understand by a "chanson vulgaire" and by "odes ou vers lyriques" when he described "Laissez la verde couleur" and the other works as "mieux dignes d'estre nommez chansons vulgaires qu'odes ou vers lyriques"?

Predictably, the passage has occasioned critical comment, often from some of the most knowledgeable students of the period. Chamard insists that Du Bellay intended an attack on Sébillet's willingness to equate chanson and ode (*Deffence*, p. 115n). The interpretation is appealing in the light of the opposition Du Bellay establishes here between ode and "chanson vulgaire," a strong echo of his preceding observation on the ode: "Sur toutes choses, prens garde que ce genre de poëme soit eloingné du vulgaire" (ed. Chamard, pp. 113-14). In Du Bellay's eyes the chanson would appear to be as closely related to what is "vulgaire" ("Vulgar, common, publicke; ordinarie, triuiall, vsuall, or much vsed," according to Cotgrave's dictionary) as the ode is not.

Prior to the publication of Brian Jeffery's *Chanson Verse of the Early Renaissance*, it would have been somewhat difficult to review a significant number of chansons in order to determine the accuracy of Du Bellay's remarks. Now, in the Jeffery volumes, which gather together all the printed chanson collections for the period c. 1512-1543, we possess ample means to grasp the common and trivial nature of the contemporary song. Even those poems whose dates place them closest in time to the period we are studying demonstrate a sustained lack of interest in a self-conscious, sophisticated diction. Most deal with love, a few with historical events, but a shift in subject matter brings about only small shifts in tone, perhaps because the same tune often served both light and serious themes. Thus, the "Chanson nouvelle faicte et composée sur les entreprinses faicte [sic] par Monsieur de Vendosme à l'encontre de ses ennemys" was to be sung to the tune of "Adieu m'amye, adieu ma rose"; moreover, its opening stanza illustrates well the level of inspiration exhibited by these poems:

> O noble seigneur de Vendosme,
> Capitaine du roy Françoys,
> A son pays de Picardie
> Tu es le chef à ceste foys.
> Prions Jesus le roy des roys
> Qu'i te doint bon commencement,
> Ainsi que tu le monstre bien
> A ton tresnoble advenement.
>
> (II, 351)

In the love poetry, the adjectives "common" and "trivial" prove even more appropriate, as poets expend their energy singing now of the deflowering of a young girl (II, 336-37), now of venereal disease (II, 345-47). Elsewhere the subject may be more lyric, but the verse no less unimpressive:

> Rossignollet, par amours je te prie
> Qu'il te plaise ung peu me resjouyr;
> Je te prometz que j'ay tresgrant desir
> D'estre à Rouen pour aller veoir m'amye.
>
> (II, 340)

The Jeffery volumes have made it possible to observe conveniently another aspect of the chanson: the evolution of its form. That some relationship between the literary chanson and the musical chanson existed over the early decades of the sixteenth century has never been doubted.[15] However, it is interesting to note at what an early date the *formes fixes* begin to fall away as privileged vehicles for lyric expression. In Jeffery's words, concerning the contents of vol. I of his edition, "The first part [chansons dated c. 1512-1525] includes some few of the older forms; those in the second part [c. 1525-1530] are all simply strophic; while many of the others in the first part are transitional" (I, 26).

Although such information underscores again the degree to which the *Deffence* misrepresents the dominant genres of the day, it also provides us with another possible means to explain Du Bellay's hostility towards the chanson. From the earliest years of the evolution away from the *formes fixes* to the publication of Sébillet's *Art poétique*, the word chanson embraced a bewildering array of texts.

Nigel Wilkins reminds us that in certain instances a rondeau by Charles d'Orléans is "called 'chanson' in the manuscript sources" (p. 141n). These rondeaux/chansons contain four stanzas. The opening lines of the first stanza close the second stanza, and the entire first stanza is repeated after the third stanza. Each stanza is composed of the same number of lines, but the arrangement of the rhymes is not uniform. In the poems by the same author entitled rondeaux, only three stanzas appear; the stanzas are not uniform in length, and only the opening line of the poem is repeated, first at the end of the second stanza and then at the close of the poem (the same rondeau form we find in Françon's edition of 600 rondeaux from Lille MS 402 and in the works of Marot).

This distinction between the rondeau/chanson and the rondeau proves to be prophetic. Because the rondeau/chanson incorporates the repeated material into its structure and makes that structure uniform, a true stanzaic work results, one separated from the new lyric form to come only by an inconsistency in the rhyme scheme of each stanza and by the long-standing practice of repeating the same rhymes throughout the poem. As Jeffery suggests, however, the emergence of the new form spans several decades.

When Fabri defines the chanson in *Le grant et vrai art de pleine rhétorique*, he insists that "combien que ballades, rondeaux, etc., se mectent en chant, si ne sont ilz pas dictz chansons, etc., car chanson est vne espece de rithme comme il s'ensuyt." Then follows this example:

> Ie chante par melencolie,
> Sans que i'aye de chanter vouloir,
> Car soulcy me faict trop doulloir
> Qui fort a sa prison me lye.
>
> Souuent i'ay ouy en ma vie
> Qu'auec les loupz il fault uller
> Et qu'en galle il se fault galler,
> Mais soulcy a sur moy enuye.
> Ie chante . . .
>
> Ma ioye est trop de moy rauie,
> S'ainsy me fault en dueil couler.
> Tristesse me vient acoller;
> Chascun de soulas me deslie.
> Ie chante, etc.
>
>   (ed. Héron, II, 94-95)

The second example contains stanzas of five lines instead of four, but in both cases the repetition of the first line of the song at the close of each stanza creates a refrain separate from the rhyme scheme of the basic stanza.

If we compare these examples of the chanson with one of the rondeaux cited by Fabri, we find distinct similarities in the use of the refrain:

> Se i'ay vostre grace requise,
> Et ma volunté s'est submise
> A vous aymer plus que nulle ame,
> Ce a esté en espoir, ma dame,
> Que mieulx vostre doulceur m'en prise
>
> Combien que soit haulte entreprise;
> Mais touteffoys, quant ie m'aduise,
> Il ne vous peult tourner a blasme,
> Se i'ay vostre grace . . .
>
> Vostre honneur point n'en amenuise.
> Vous n'en debuez estre reprise,
> Se moy ou vng aultre vous ame;

Et ia n'en perdrez sur mon ame
Vostre liberté et franchise,
Se i'ay . . .

(ed. Héron, II, 66)

The refrain is again provided by the poem's first line, and it is repeated in the same places as in the chanson. Judging by the difference in length between the first and last stanzas, we could also conclude that, as with the chanson, the refrain constitutes an added line and that the difference for Fabri between the chanson and the rondeau lies in the stanzaic structure. All stanzas in the chanson are of the same length. Only the first and third stanzas of the rondeau are equal in length.

These examples show us just how diverse were the notions abroad in the world of poetry concerning the chanson. The form to which the Charles d'Orléans manuscripts attach the term announces the future ode, that is, a poem of uniform stanzas without a refrain that is appended to each stanza. The Fabri examples combine the chanson/ode model with the refrain of the rondeau. Thanks to the contents of Jeffery's edition, we discover that despite such complexity the history of the chanson embraces both early and substantial progress.

Jeffery's first volume, representing in the main chanson verse before 1530, leaves no doubt that poets familiar with the musical chanson[16] made important strides in developing the chanson/ode form. Already the first title whose contents are reproduced, *S'ensuivent plusieurs belles chansons nouvelles*, dated c. 1515-1520, shows us a "chanson de verdellet" comprising nine quatrains, all rhymed abba, with no refrain and no rhymes repeated throughout the poem (I, 52-53). Similarly, a "chanson nouvelle sur 'Vive L'Espiciere'" proves to be composed of six heterometric huitains rhymed ababbcbc with, again, no refrain and no rhymes repeated in each stanza, although the rhyme scheme of the fifth stanza is slightly defective (I, 72-73). "Vray dieu d'amours" presents five quatrains with no refrain. Each quatrain is rhymed aaab. The b rhyme remains constant in each stanza, but no a rhyme reappears throughout the poem (I, 76).

To be sure, these harbingers of new lyric forms to come are surrounded by other works less easily classified. "En plains et pleurs je prens congé" contains six septains, all rhymed ababbcc, with a refrain as the final verse of every stanza, much like the ballade style (I, 50-51).[17] However, each stanza contains a separate set of rhymes. Experimentation continues into the period when Saint-Gelais's earliest published works appear. His "Description d'Amour," for example, was first printed with other contemporary poems under the rubric "Les Fleurs de poésie françoyse," a subheading of a volume entitled *Hecatomphile*. In the preceding chapter, I commented on the telling proportion of *formes fixes* to epigrams found in "Les Fleurs." The structure of the longer poems included in "Les Fleurs" proves to be no less telling.

"Merueille n'est qu'amour plus que mort furieux" (pp. 72-73) is printed with no break in its sixteen lines. It would thus seem to be a poem in the vein of the opening selection which grows ever longer through the continued multiplication of its rhymes (ababbcbccbcbcbcdedeedede). In truth, "Merueille n'est" is constructed very differently. The rhyme scheme reveals it to be divided into two stanzas with a concluding segment somewhat shorter in length than the preceding "stanzas" (quite in the mode of the envoi of a ballade). However, there is no refrain, and, although the rhyme scheme is identical in the two "stanzas," no rhyme is repeated in the second "stanza": ababab[/] cdcdcd[/]cece. More striking still are two of the three final poems of the collection.

In "Quand le corps iustement reçoit punition" (p. 99), we find five heterometric stanzas on the pattern aaab bbbc cccd ddde eeef. Not only is each quatrain structured in the same way, but, since a, c and e are masculine rhymes and b, d and f feminine rhymes, "Quand le corps" provides a very early example of both similarly structured stanzas and the alternation of masculine and feminine rhymes.

The last work in "Les Fleurs," "Adam fut faict & formé Gentilhomme" (pp. 100-03), is reminiscent of "Merueille n'est" in that it, too, contains a series of stanzas based on a repeated rhyme scheme[18] (but with no repetition of any rhyme), followed by a quatrain. Here, however, the poet accumulates no fewer than nine septains (now typographically delineated), of decasyllabic lines.

Of such trends within the world of chanson verse, Du Bellay could not have been unaware. After all, "imperfect" chansons continued to be published on the very eve of the *Deffence*.

In the 1548 *Chansons nouvellement composées sur plusieurs chants, tant de musique que rustique*, although a stanzaic form is generally indicated, there seems to be little regularity among the stanzas of more than one poem. The second contains two quatrains, the first in *rimes embrassées*, the second in *rimes croisées*. The third poem is composed of nine sizains with a bewildering array of rhyme schemes, no two of which appear in successive stanzas. The next song, "Amours, amours," consists of five dizains. Some patterns are discernible—lines 5 and 6 rhyme in all but one stanza, lines 8 and 9 rhyme in all stanzas—but there is no consistency with regard to which rhyme within each stanza repeats in those lines.

The same anthology reminds us that poets and printers concerned with the chanson could be careless with content as well as with prosody. A version of "O combien est heureuse" (reproduced below, p. 54) appears in the *Chansons nouvellement composées*. Saint Gelais's poem has been severely recast, and the result is not always intelligible. Consider the new opening stanza:

> Or combien est heureuse la peine de celuy:
> Dune femme amoureuse / qui deux cueurs faict brusler
> Quant chascun deulx sentend destre content.

"Celer" has been changed to "celuy," "Une" to "Dune," "flamme" to "femme," "s'attend" to "sentend," and the poet's original statement is no longer recognizable.

Not all chanson verse of the day presents a text that is either incomprehensible or technically imperfect. Some poems give evidence rather of a lack of polish at the level of both style and prosody, as can be seen from the chansons spirituelles included by Marguerite de Navarre in her *Marguerites* of 1547. Dottin's critical apparatus to his edition of these chansons calls attention to weaknesses in the rhymes (p. xlviii), use of familiar, popular language despite the religious themes explored (p. lxii), and to echoes of facile alliteration in the mode of the Rhétoriqueurs (pp. xlviii-xlix).[19] Others' songs merit use of the adjective "vulgaire" because of their obscene content, a quality that has been noted by various musicologists,[20] and one that Laumonier may well have had in mind when he equated Du Bellay's phrase "chansons vulgaires" with the "chanson marotique," that is, with a love poem written in stanzas and ranging in tone from light-hearted treatment of courtly themes to thinly veiled obscenity.[21] If such was Du Bellay's meaning, we are, unfortunately, no closer to explaining his attack on the three poems he mentions than when we observe to what degree contemporary chanson verse was often imperfect, inelegant or ill defined.

Not one of the three chansons dismissed by Du Bellay fails to maintain the same rhyme pattern in every stanza. Even the rhymes employed, if we use as a basis for comparison Dottin's examples of "négligences" in Marguerite's chansons ("rimes verbales," "rimes du simple et du composé," "rimes du suffixe," "rimes de termes homophones," "antonymes," "la rime d'un mot avec lui-même," p. xlviii), serve to distinguish the poems from the more crudely crafted chansons of the time. Such "négligences" do appear, but the frequency is too small to be of any consequence.

More significant yet is the fact that "Laissez la verde couleur," "Amour avecques Psyches" and "O combien est heureuse" all fall into the pattern of the chanson/ode, even though, quite in keeping with the thrust of Fabri's treatise, poets of the 1540s composed chansons that contained stanzas of uniform length, but with refrains added. One of Marguerite's chansons spirituelles even recalls Fabri's examples, that is, chanson verse in which the refrain, rondeau-like, derives from the first line of the poem:

> A Dieu pour tout jamais, A Dieu.
> En l'ignorance du matin,
> Sans voir du vray Soleil le jour,
> De plaisir j'entre au Jardin
> Plein d'honneur et biens à l'entour,
> Pour jamais n'en faire retour;
> Mais j'y trouvé la mort pour jeu.
>   A Dieu.
>   (ed. Dottin, p. 56)

To espy the difference in form between such chansons and the three works he dismisses, Du Bellay would not have had to look beyond the poems reproduced by Du Moulin with "Laissez la verde couleur." Several make use of a refrain either in the form of lines repeated after each stanza ("Dames sçauriez vous," 1545, sig. b1r) or through repetition of the same line as the concluding verse of each stanza ("Nonobstant sa grand cruauté," sig. b5r; "Quand vne Dame," sig. b5v; "Qui celera laffection," sig. b6r). At least one poem contains an irregular rhyme scheme.[22] It is true, of course, that "Laissez la verde couleur," with its use of the same rhyme for the second and fourth lines of every stanza, departs slightly from the pattern which the ode will follow,[23] but the poems it is coupled with by Du Bellay do not.

Similarly, none of the poems ventures into the ribald or the obscene. "O combien est heureuse" contains throughout a style removed from the "rare & antique erudition" that Du Bellay demanded for the ode, but we may profitably ask whether, as a result, this characteristic stanza,

> Si femme en ma presence
> Autre vous entretient,
> Amour veult que je pense
> Que cela m'appartient,
> Car luy et longue foy
> Vous doivent tout à moy
> (vv. 25-30)

shares nothing of consequence with these stanzas included by Du Bellay in an ode from his *Vers lyriques* of 1549:

> Par ce petit Dieu puissant,
> Delaissant
> Le doulx gyron de la mere,
> La vierge femme se treuve,
> Et fait preuve
> De la flamme doulceamere.
>
> Que me chaut si on le blasme,
> Et sa flamme?
> Amour ne scait abuser:

> Et ceux qui mal en recoyvent,
> Ne le doyvent,
> Mais eux mesmes, accuser.
> (*Oeuvres*, III, 14)

The case of "Laissez la verde couleur" is even more interesting. Not only does an elegant and elevated style pertain throughout, raising the poem well above the conventional (but decidedly not "common" language of "O combien est heureuse"), but we also find in the work examples of the very erudition Du Bellay required in an ode: use of "Cytheree" and "Cypris" (for Venus), references to Myrrha, the Elysian Fields, Troy, Juno and the judgment of Paris. In addition, we are offered one extended comparison (vv. 37-44), sententious phrasing (vs. 111), significant variation in the rhetoric of Venus' lament (cf. vv. 79, 81, 91, 93), elements appearing in verses without an equivalent in the poet's sources and attributable, therefore, to Saint-Gelais's own imagination.

Other signs of a desire on Saint-Gelais's part to make "Laissez la verde couleur" an impressive piece were not available to the poets at Coqueret when they formulated the *Deffence*. Certain variants (see below, pp. 46-49) intimate that "Laissez la verde couleur" was on more than one occasion reread and revised.

An initial examination of these variants raises the possibility that the version of the poem printed by Du Moulin could have been only a faulty copy of the work. After all, the disagreement that occurs in vv. 32, 40, 43 and 71 between the Du Moulin text and nearly every subsequent printing (as well as the two manuscripts collated) would suggest such a conclusion. On the other hand, other manuscript variants sometimes agree with each other, but not with the printed versions, including Du Moulin's (cf. vv. 12, 75, 79, 107, 117, 124, 145, 156). As a result, it would seem rather incautious to isolate Du Moulin's text from among the other texts of the poem or to consider it inauthentic. The readings it offers for vv. 32, 40 and 71 are no more, no less unique than the manuscript variants just referred to.

Although Saint-Gelais has left us no means to determine the precise relationship among the various versions of his poem, the history of "Laissez la verde couleur" does underscore one clear fact: the readings unique to Du Moulin and the two manu-scripts disappear after 1545 from the ensuing editions of the poem (if we except the *Discours* of 1546 and *Le Livre de plu-sieurs pièces* of 1548, which give every indication of having taken their text of the poem from Du Moulin's edition). We can only guess at the reasons why certain variants were preferred, but if there is any substance to our guesses, they do speak well for Saint-Gelais.

Here are vv. 37-40 of "Laissez la verde couleur" as they ap-peared in Du Moulin's first printing of the poem:

> Mais comme une rose blanche,
> De poignante ongle touchee,
> Ne peut tenir sur la branche,
> Mais sur une autre est couchee.

Although all later printings do not change "Ne peut tenir sur la branche" to "sur sa branche" (whereas vs. 40 appears regularly after 1545 as "Et sur une autre est couchee"), the variants in question imply that at some point Saint-Gelais reviewed the passage with regard to euphony and sense. "Sa," more than "la," accentuates the desired distinction between the two phases of the rose's existence; "Et," in lieu of "Mais," avoids repetition of the conjunction that begins the quatrain.

Even more suggestive is the variant for vs. 43. The 1545 text gives the reading "Comme s'il estoit dormant." Subsequent editions print "Comme il souloit en dormant." Du Moulin's original version comes very close to the Greek model: "même mort il est beau dans la mort, comme s'il reposait" (vs. 71). However, another quatrain also indicates that Adonis in death gives the appearance of being asleep:

> Et ne fust le sang qui sort
> De la partie entamee,
> Elle penseroit qu'il dort
> A sa grace tant aymee.
> (vv. 45-48)

The variant for vs. 43 moves us farther from the Greek source, but also insures that the same image no longer appears in two nearly contiguous quatrains.

Perceptive readers of "Laissez la verde couleur" will have noted that, in one respect at least, Saint-Gelais produced an "imperfect" poem. The work fails to alternate masculine and feminine rhymes, a trait for which *Les Recherches* roundly scoulds the poet: "La plus belle chanson que fit Melin de Sainct Gelais, est celle qui se commence: *Laissez la verte couleur, ô Princesse Cytherée*. En laquelle vous ne trouuerez aucun ordre des masculins & feminins . . . . Qui est vne grande faute aux Chansons, qui doiuent passer par la mesure d'vne mesme musique" (p. 627). Pasquier's thoughts notwithstanding, "Laissez la verde couleur" was set to music by no fewer than five composers, and Saulnier chides Pasquier for his obvious error.[24] However, had Saulnier consulted the text of the four vocal settings of the poem, he would have found that the latest in date, the text published by Jean Chardavoine in the *Recueil des plus belles et excellentes chansons* (1576), is a much revised version of the poem. All quatrains that originally neglected to alternate masculine and feminine rhymes, if retained by the composer, undergo a recasting and emerge with an unerring mfmf rhyme scheme.[25]

Thus, Pasquier's view gradually did become law; it cannot have been so in the 1540s, and, in addition to "Laissez la verde couleur," we have as proof of that fact the "Au Lecteur" written by Du Bellay to introduce his *Vers lyriques* of 1549: "Je n'ay (Lecteur) entremellé fort supersticieusement les vers masculins avecques les feminins, comme on use en ces vaudevilles, & chansons qui se chantent d'un mesme chant part tous les coupletz, craignant de contreindre & gehinner ma diction pour l'observation de telles choses" (*Oeuvres*, III, 3).[26] By Du Bellay's own admission, the "failure" of Saint-Gelais and Pernette to alternate masculine and feminine rhymes in their poems could not be held against them, and we are foiled again in an attempt to pinpoint the source of Du Bellay's animosity. The actual reasons stated in the *Deffence* mislead in that they prove representative of many contemporary chansons, but not those cited by Du Bellay. In the last analysis, the desire of the young poets at Coqueret to discredit, and dissociate themselves from, the verse of the day becomes our surest explanation for Du

Bellay's words, even though the very popularity achieved by the three poems would have permitted readers then as now to grasp the unfairness of the attack. Still, no one has ever maintained that the *Deffence* was a carefully executed work. In these and other pages the thrust of the poets' sentiments emerges with a clarity that, unfortunately, was not imposed upon the accompanying discussion.

At the same time, our investigation of Du Bellay's attitude towards "Laissez la verde couleur" and the two other poems has opened up more than one avenue to explore if we are to understand better Mellin's place in literary history: a long-standing evolution in lyric poetry away from the *formes fixes*, an appreciation for Saint-Gelais in the world of neo-Latin verse, a concern on the part of Saint-Gelais well in advance of the *Deffence* for crafted and elegant poetry modeled on classical sources of impeccable reputation. It is, therefore, to a pursuit of these facets of our subject that we turn now.

A. "Laissez la verde couleur"
Text and Variants

The text reproduced below is that of the first printing of the poem by Antoine Du Moulin (Lyon, 1545) with two emendations (vv. 3 and 126) where the 1545 edition contains evident errors. The punctuation has been modernized, abbreviations resolved, and the distinctions between i and j, u and v introduced. Also, a few accents have been added for clarity; otherwise, the text appears as it did in 1545.

Of the 1545 volume, P.A. Becker has written: "1545 veröffentlichte Antoine du Moulin unter dem Titel *Deploration sur la mort du bel Adonis avec plusieurs autres compositions nouvelles* (Lyon, Jean de Tournes) die Chanson *Laissez la verde couleur* . . . mit den Initialen S.-G. und die *Complainte amoureuse* in Terze rime . . . neben einer Menge andere Kompositionen . . ." (p. 39). This description differs in several ways from the Houghton Library copy, catalogued *FC5 D8994. 545d. The Houghton volume bears the title *Déploration de Vénus sur la mort du bel Adonis avec plusieurs autres compositions nouvelles.* The initials S.-G. are nowhere present, and no *Complainte* in terza rima appears. As the Cartier/Chennevière study of Du Moulin makes clear that the *Complainte* in question constitutes one of the texts Du Moulin added later to the poems published in 1545 when he reprinted the *Déploration* [*RHLF*, 3 (1896), p. 98], it seems questionable that Becker ever saw a copy of the 1545 volume.

Under the heading of "Variants" the reader will find recorded a wide variety of alternate forms. Some are evident typographical errors, rather than variants in the strictest sense of the term, but all aid us in identifying characteristics of the several editions of the poems and, in certain cases, in tracing the influence of one printing upon a later reissue of the same poem.

Déploration du bel Adonis

"Laissez la verde couleur,
    O Princesse Cytheree,
    Et de nouvelle douleur
    Vostre beaulté soit paree.
5   Plourez le filz de Myrrha
    Et sa dure destinee.
    Vostre œil plus ne le voirra,
    Car sa vie est terminee."
Venus, à celle nouvelle,
10   Remplit toute la vallee
    D'une complaincte mortelle,
    Et au lieu s'en est allee
Où le gentil Adonis,
    Estendu sur la rosee,
15   Avoit ses beaux yeux ternis
    Et de sang l'herbe arrosee.
Dessoubz une verde branche
    Aupres de luy s'est couchee,
    Et de sa belle main blanche
20   Sa playe luy ha touchee.
O nouvelle cruaulté,
    De veoir en pleurs si baignee
    La Deesse de beaulté
    D'amy mort accompaignee.
25   L'un est blessé et transfix
    Aux flans par beste insensee,
    Et l'autre l'est de son Filz
    Bien avant dans la pensee.
Mais l'un sa playe ne sent,
30   Personne jà trespassee,
    Et l'autre ha le mal recent
    De la douleur amassee.
Toutesfois de mort attaint
    Il n'ha de rien empiree

35   La grand' beaulté de son taint
       Des Nymphes tant desiree.
Mais comme une rose blanche,
       De poignante ongle touchee,
       Ne peut tenir sur la branche,
40   Mais sur une autre est couchee,
Ainsi le piteux Amant
       Avoit la teste appuyee,
       Comme s'il estoit dormant
       Sur sa maistresse ennuyee.
45   Et ne fust le sang qui sort
       De la partie entamee,
       Elle penseroit qu'il dort
       A sa grace tant aymee.
Autant de sang qu'il espand
50   Dessus l'herbe couloree,
       Autant de larmes respand
       La povre Amante esploree.
Le sang rougist mainte fleur
       Qui blanche estoit autour nee,
55   Et mainte est de large pleur
       En couleur blanche tournee.
Ce taint leur demourera
       Pour enseigne de duree
       Tant que le monde sera
60   De leur grand peine enduree.
Là vindrent de tous les Boys
       Oyseaux par grande assemblee,
       Monstrans à leur triste voix
       Combien leur joye est troublee.
65   Mais sur tous se faict ouyr
       La povre desesperee,
       Qui pour d'Adonis jouyr
       Se souhaite estre expiree.
"O Deité trop cruelle,
70   O vie trop obstinee,
       Comment ne m'as-tu," dict-elle,
       "Une fin predestinee?
O demeure du Ciel tiers
       Par moy jadis tant prisee,
75   Combien et plus voulentiers
       J'yrois au champ Elysee.

A la fille de Ceres
    Est ma joye abandonnee.
    O, qu'heureuse je serois
80   D'estre en sa place ordonnee.
Vienne le grand ravisseur
    De l'infernale contree,
    Il pourra bien estre seur
    D'avoir faveur rencontree.
85   Las, que le Ciel ne m'octroye
    Pouvoir morte estre laissee,
    Aussi bien que devant Troye
    Il me souffrit veoir blessee.
Si je puis lors estre ainsi
90   Par dure playe offensee,
    Pourquoy ne peulx-je estre aussi
    Par mort de dueil dispensee?
N'ayez plus sur moy d'envie,
    Royne du Ciel honoree.
95   Puisqu'Adonis est sans vie,
    Peu vault ma Pomme doree.
Las, tant ne me contentois
    De me la veoir adjugee;
    Comme heureuse me sentois
100   D'estre en si bon cœur logee.
Et vous, povres chiens lassés,
    Bestes d'amour asseuree,
    Sans seigneur estes laissés,
    Moy, sans Amy demouree.
105   Bien pourrez recouvrer maistre,
    Aymant la chasse usitee,
    Et m'amour ne pourroit estre
    Autre part resuscitee.
De course legere et prompte,
110   Suyviez la beste lancee,
    Mais Fortune qui tout dompte
    S'est plus que vous avancee.
O violent animal!
    O fureur desavouee!
115   Comme ozas-tu faire mal
    A chose à Venus vouee?
Comme ne peult s'appaiser
    Ta dent par ire accrochee,

     Venant attaindre et baiser
120   Beauté des Dieux approchee?
Et vous, Amy trop espris
    De vostre force esprouvee,
    Si mon conseil eussiez pris,
    Mieux je m'en fusse trouvee.
125 Cerfs, Dains, et bestes fuyantes
    Estoyent mieux vostre portee
    Que les fieres et bruyantes
    Qui m'ont tant desconfortee.
Qu'aviez-vous à faire queste
130   D'autre proye pourchassee?
    Estoit-ce peu de conqueste
    De m'avoir prinse et lassee?"
Ainsi faisant tristes plains,
    Cypris, d'espoir desnuee,
135   Leva ses yeux d'humeur plains
    Vers le cler Ciel sans nuee
Et vit le Soleil couchant
    Mettant fin à sa journee.
    Si feit un souspir trenchant
140   Et vers le mort s'est tournee,
Disant, "Las, l'heure est venue
    Que toute chose créee
    De sa peine soustenue
    Dormant sera recréee.
145 Mais pour moy les jours et nuictz
    N'ont point d'heure disposee
    A terminer mes ennuictz
    Et me trouver reposee."
Au son de ses cris indignes
150   Respond Echo tourmentee,
    Et mesmes ses deux blancz Cygnes
    Chanson piteuse ont chantee.
Mais voyant l'obscure nuict
    Estre jà presque arrivee,
155   Ont doulcement et sans bruit
    Leur maistresse en l'air levee.
Plus elle approche des Cieulx,
    Plus tient la teste baissee,
    Et eust voulentiers ses yeulx
160   Et sa veuë en bas laissee.

Variants

Siglum	Text Collated
M	Musée Condé, Chantilly, MS 523.
M_1	MS B.N. n.a. fr. 1158.
A	Du Moulin, Antoine, *Déploration de Vénus sur la mort du bel Adonis*, Lyon, 1545.
B	La Borderie, Le Seigneur de, *Le Discours du voyage de Constantinople*, Paris, 1546.
C	Saint-Gelais, Mellin de, *Saingelais, Oeuvres de luy tant en composition que translation, ou allusion aux auteurs grecs et latins*, Lyon, 1547.
A_1	Du Moulin, Antoine, *Déploration de Vénus sur la mort du bel Adonis*, Lyon 1547.
A_2	Du Moulin, Antoine, *Déploration de Vénus sur la mort du bel Adonis*, Lyon, 1548.
B_1	*Le Livre de plusieurs pièces*, Lyon, 1548.
D	*Recueil des chansons, tant musicales que rurales, anciennes et modernes, par le moyen desquelles on pourra facilement apprendre la poësie et stile de composer en rime françoise*, Paris, n.d. [cited in British Museum catalogue as "1550?"].
E	Certon, Pierre, *Premier Livre de chansons, en quatre volumes*, Paris, 1552.
A_3	Du Moulin, Antoine, *Déploration de Vénus sur la mort du bel Adonis*, Ghent?, 1554. [Although the Arsenal catalogue lists the volume as "Gand, 1554," the title page says only that the book may be purchased there: "On les vend à Gand chez Girard de Salenson deuant l'hostel de la ville à l'enseigne de la Bible . . . ." No explicit place of publication is given.]
F	*Le Recueil de toutes les sortes de chansons nouvelles, rustiques et musicales, et aussi ceulx qui sont dans la déploration de Vénus*, Lyon, 1555.
A_4	Du Moulin, Antoine, *Déploration de Vénus sus la mort du bel Adonis*, Lyon, 1556.
A_5	Du Moulin, Antoine, *La Déploration de Vénus sur la mort du bel Adonis*, Paris, 1561.
G	Le Roy, Adrian, *Premier Livre de chansons en forme de vau de ville*, Paris, 1573.
C_1	Saint-Gelais, Mellin de, *Oeuvres poétiques de Mellin de S. Gelais*, Lyon, 1574.

H   Chardavoine, Jean, *Le Recueil des plus belles et excellentes chansons*, Paris, 1576.

The Albert Seay edition of Jacob Arcadelt's *Collected Works* states that beginning in 1561 Arcadelt published text and music for "Laissez la verde couleur" (9, xiv). I have not been able to locate a copy of the 1561 Arcadelt volume. Since the text reproduced by Seay contains only 24 verses of the poem (9, 25-27), I have not added it to the collation. It is worth noting, however, that in the portion of the poem quoted by Seay no alternation of masculine and feminine rhymes is imposed on the work.

verse 3	A	couleur
4	A_5	no punctuation at end
5	H	period at end
6	A_5	no punctuation at end
7	A_3	oel
8	H	no punctuation at end
9	F	period at end
9-11	H	oyant ces propos / D'vn cry remplist la vallee / Et sans nul repos
11	F	period at end
12	M, M_1	Et droi[c]t au lieu est allee; H Droict au lieu; B, C, B_1, E, F, A_5, G period at end
13	A_2	gentit; H gemil
15	F, H	Auoir; M les; A_5 period at end
17	H	l'ombre des rameaux
18	M_1	fut couchee
19	H	ses doigts si tres beaux
20	F	à
21	M	O cruelle nouueaulte; A_5 nonuelle
22	A_5	en plusieurs; M, M_1, F, H pleur
25	M	blece; B_1 blesse; F blese; H blecé; A_5 transi; H tranfix
26	M_1	A mort par; F Au
28	M	en; M_1, G en sa; C_1 dans sa
29	H	sens
30	H	trespasée
31	G	à
32	M, M_1, C, A_1, A_2, D, E, A_3, F, A_4, A_5, G, C_1, H sa		

33   M, M_1 mort et estainct

35   A_5 tant

37   H   blanche fleur

38   M_1 poignant; F   couchee

39   M, M_1, C, A_1, A_2, A_3, A_4, G   sa; H   Se panche & perd sa
          couleur

40   M, M_1, C, A_1, A_2, E, A_3, F, A_4, A_5, G, C_1 Et; D   Ains; H
          Dessus vn autre; B, C, B_1, D, E, A_5, G   period at end

42   M_1, C, A_1, A_2, E, A_3, A_4, G, C_1 Tenoit sa; D, F, A_5, H
          Tenoit la; M   Baisse la

43   M, M_1, C, A_1, A_2, D, E, A_3, F, A_4, A_5, G, C_1, H   il souloit
          en

44   F   Sus

47   H   Lon diroit presque; M_1 jugeroyt

48   M   la

51   H   les larmes; M_1 lhermes despand; E   l'armes espend;
          M   despend; G   espand

52   M, G   triste

54   M   dautre sorte estoit

55   M, H   du

57   H   demeurra

61   F   La; M   tout le bois; B, B_1 Roys

62   M, M_1 a grande; B_1 grand'; E, G   à grande; A_5 grand

63   B_1, D, E, F, A_4, A_5, G, H   Monstrant; F   leurs; M, M_1, C
          leurs tristes

65   C, A_1, A_2, A_3, A_4, C_1, H   tout

67   M   Adonis

68   A_5 expire, no punctuation at end

69   A_5 O biere; H   O cruelle deité; C   period at end

70   M_1 O pitie; H   ostinee

71   M, M_1, C, A_1, A_2, D, A_3, F, A_4, A_5, C_1 Las que nay je ce
          dit elle; H   Las que n'aye en limité

72   D, A_5 period at end; H   comma at end

73   A_4 Du

74   M, M_1 De moy

75   M, M_1 Combien [h]or

76   M   Irois je; M_1, E, F   Yrois; D   aux champs d'Elisée; H
          aux champs d'Helisee

78   A_5 no punctuation at end

79   M, M_1 Ha que; F   eureuse

80   H   a sa; A_5 no punctuation at end

85   A_5 mettoye; H   vv. 85-92 omitted

86   A5   Pouruoir; F   lassee
87   A5   period at end
88   A5   no punctuation at end
89   A5   Sire ie
90   A5   no punctuation at end
91   A5   il
92   B1   par ma mort; F   period at end; A5   no punctuation
           at end
93   H   N'ayez plus sur moy courroux
94   M, M1   O Royne au; B1   period at end
95   M, M1   Puis que; H   Puisqu'est mort mon amy doux
96   A5   Peult, bonne, no punctuation at end
97   H   tans
98   M, M1, H   De la me; H   voit
99   M1   je seroys
100   H   si omitted
101   A5   nous
103   B1   seigneurs; B   lassez
104   A5   no punctuation at end
105   A5   maistre printed upside down; H   vous maistre auoir
106   F, A5   visitee
107   M, M1   scauroit; D   Mais; H   Mais mamour ne pouray voir
108   M1   En aultre; C, A1, A2, D, A3, F, A4, A5, C1, H   En
           autruy; A5   no punctuation at end
109   A5   leger; H   De caurse legere au vent
110   B1, H   Suyuez; D, F, A5   Suyurez
111   H   poursuiuant
112   A5   no punctuation at end
113   A5   no punctuation at end
114   M1   desordonnee; A5   no punctuation at end
116   A5   no punctuation at end
117   M, M1   Com[m]ent
118   A5   par omitted; H   vv. 118-21 omitted
119   M1   & blessee
120   A   comma at end; C, A1   period at end
122   A5   no punctuation at end
124   M, M1   Elle sen fust myeulx trouuee; F   question mark at
           end
125   H   Cerfs dains animaux fuyans
126   M1, A, B   Estoit
127   H   cruels & bruyans
128   H   Qui tant m'ont; A5   no punctuation at end

129	H	vv. 129-32 omitted
130	A	comma at end; B colon at end; A_5 no punctuation at end
132	M	lacee; D laissée; F no punctuation at end; A_5 period at end
133	M_1	En faisant ces; C_1 triste
134	M_1	Le pris; B_1 Cy pris; F period at end
135	F, A_4, A_5, C_1, H	humeurs
136	B, B_1	le ciel cler; H crel; A_5 nu
137	F	souleil
138	M, M_1, C, A_1, A_2, D, A_3, F, A_4, A_5, C_1, H	la; A_5 no punctuation at end
140	M_1, A_1, A_3, A_5	la mort; H c'est
141	D	las omitted
141-44	H	or est le seiour / De la nuicteuse vespree / Que de la peine du iour / Chacun dormant se recree
142	B_1, D, F	crée; A_5 cree
144	B_1, D, F	recrée; A_5 recree
145	M, M_1	Et pour
146	H	composee
148	D, F, A_5	disposée; H Et me trouue disposee; A_5 no punctuation at end
149	H	piteux
151	H	Et ses blanc Cignes tous deux
152	A_5	on
154	H	ta
156	M, M_1	Leur dame en lair esleuee; F no punctuation at end
158	A_5	tien; M_1 sa
159	A_5	les; F period at end

B. "O combien est heureuse"
Text and Variants

The text reproduced below is again that of the first printing of the poem by Antoine Du Moulin (Lyon, 1545) with one emendation (vs. 24) where a clear typographical error appears. As with "Laissez la verde couleur," the punctuation has been

modernized, abbreviations resolved, and the distinctions between
i and j, u and v introduced.

Chanson par une Dame

O combien est heureuse
   La peine de celer
   Une flamme amoureuse
   Qui deux cueurs faict brusler
5   Quand chascun d'eulx s'attend
   D'estre bien tost content.
Las, on veult que je taise
   Mon apparent desir,
   En faignant qu'il me plaise
10   Nouvel amy choisir.
   Mais telle fiction
   Veult mesme affection.
Vostre amour froide et lente
   Vous rend ainsi discret;
15   La mienne violente
   N'entend pas ce secret.
   Amour nulle saison
   N'est amy de raison.
Si mon feu sans fumee
20   Est evident et chault,
   Estant de vous aymee,
   Du reste ne m'enchault.
   Soit mon mal veu de tous
   Et seul senty de vous.
25 Si femme en ma presence
   Autre vous entretient,
   Amour veult que je pense
   Que cela m'appartient,
   Car luy et longue foy
30   Vous doivent tout à moy.
Que me sert que je soye
   Avec Princes ou Roy,
   Et qu'ailleurs je vous voye
   Sans approcher de moy?
35   La peur du changement
   Me cause grand tourment.

Quand par bonne fortune
    Serez mien à tout poinct,
    Lors parlez à chascune;
40   Je ne m'en plaindray point.
    Bien vous pry ce pendant
    N'estre ailleurs pretendant.
Helas, qu'il fust possible
    Que tu puisse estre moy,
45   Pour veoir si m'est penible
    Le mal que j'ay pour toy.
    Tu prendrois grand pitié
    De ma ferme amytié.
Vous semble que la veuë
50   Soit assez entre amys,
    Ne me voyant pourveuë
    De ce qu'on m'ha promis?
    C'est trop peu que des yeulx.
    Amour veult avoir mieulx.
55 De vous seul je confesse
    Que mon cueur est transi.
    Si j'estois grand princesse,
    Je dirois tout alnsi.
    Si le vostre ainsi faict,
60   Monstrez-le par effect.

Variants

Siglum	Text Collated
A	Du Moulin, Antoine, *Déploration de Vénus sur la mort du bel Adonis*, Lyon, 1545.
B	La Borderie, Le Seigneur de, *Le Discours du voyage de Constantinople*, Paris, 1546.
C	Saint-Gelais, Mellin de, *Saingelais, Oeuvres de luy tant en composition que translation, ou allusion aux auteurs grecs et latins*, Lyon, 1547.
A₁	Du Moulin, Antoine, *Déploration de Vénus sur la mort du bel Adonis*, Lyon, 1547.
D	Sébillet, Thomas, *Art poétique françois*, Paris, 1548.
A₂	Du Moulin, Antoine, *Déploration de Vénus sur la mort du bel Adonis*, Lyon, 1548.

B$_1$	*Le Livre de plusieurs pièces*, Lyon, 1548.
E	Certon, Pierre, *Premier Livre de chansons*, Paris, 1552.
A$_3$	Du Moulin, Antoine, *Déploration de Vénus sur la mort du bel Adonis*, Ghent?, 1554.
A$_4$	Du Moulin, Antoine, *Déploration de Vénus sus la mort du bel Adonis*, Lyon, 1556.
M	MS B.N. fr. 885. [Since this manuscript contains poetry written for court events that took place in 1557, it cannot have been produced prior to that date.]
A$_5$	Du Moulin, Antoine, *La Déploration de Vénus sur la mort du bel Adonis*, Paris, 1561.
F	Le Roy, Adrian, *Premier Livre de chansons en forme de vau de ville*, Paris, 1573.
G	Chardavoine, Jean, *Le Recueil des plus belles et excellentes chansons*, Paris 1576.

verse 2	A, B, E, F comma after peine; A$_5$ period at end; G comma at end
4	G coeur
5	G Qand
6	A$_4$, M Estre
7	C, M On me di[c]t; A$_4$ Lon me dit
9	C Et; D, A$_4$, M Et feigne; A$_5$ baise
10	G omy
11	D, M forte affection
12	D N'endure fiction; M n'a point de fiction; A$_5$ no punctuation at end
13	A$_3$ froid; M foible; G froiée; C stanzas 3 and 4 are printed in reverse order
14	M fait; D sage & discret; A$_5$ no punctuation at end
15	G volonte
16	G pes; C, A$_4$ point; A$_5$ le, no punctuation at end
17	A$_5$ Amors
18	B, B$_1$ amye; A$_5$ comma at end
20	D uiolent
22	B, D, B$_1$, A$_4$, M, G il ne; C D'aultres il ne; B, C, A$_1$, A$_2$, B$_1$, E, A$_3$, A$_5$, F m'en chault; D, A$_4$, M, G me chaut; A$_5$ no punctuation at end
23	M feu
24	A, A$_1$, A$_2$, A$_3$ sentu; A$_5$ sent tu, comma at end

25   M   reverses order of next two stanzas
26   A5   Autre que vous; G   Aures
29   A5   period at end
30   C   tous; D   a; A5   no punctuation at end
31   C   stanza printed as last stanza; A5   Qui
32   C, D   Auecque Prince; M   Prince; A4   Auecques Prince; A5
        Prince & Roy; F   Rois
33   A5   prie
34   A5   comma at end
35   A4   de; A5   Voit la peur du changement, period at end
36   C   se tourment; A4, M   donne; G   donue
37   A5   Quaud, par omitted; G   fourrune
38   G   Sera; C, D, E, M, F, G   de; A5   tous poinctz; G   tont
39   D   a; C   chescune; G   parler
40   C   Il ne m'en chauldra; G   Il m'en chaudra point
41   C, D   le uous; A5   prie
43   C, D, A4, M   stanza omitted; C   stanza "De vous seul" placed
        here
44   A1, A2, E, A3, A5, F   Que puisses; A5, F   à moy; G   puissiez
        lire en moy
45   F   s'il; A5   possible; G   le mal penible
46   A5   no punctuation at end; G   Que pour vous ie reçoy
47   G   Vous auriez
48   A5   comma at end
49   B, A1, A2, B1, E, A3, A4, A5, M, F, G   semble il; D   Pensez
        uous
51   C   Ie ne me sens
52   C   Du bien; A4, M   De rien qu'on m'ait promis; A, A1, A3
        period at end; A5   comma at end; G   colon at end
53   G   tes; A5   no punctuation at end
55   C   Pour
56   C   Mon coeur estre; D, A5   comma at end
57   G   S'il estois; E, F   i'estoye; A5   comma after grand; B, C,
        A1, A2, B1, A3, A4   grand'
58   E, F   Ie le diroye; G   Ie le dirois ainsi

Two volumes of sixteenth-century chansons contain versions
of this poem. As each departs in numerous verses from the standard text, it seems best to reproduce the poems *in toto*, separate
from the variants printed above.

From *Chansons nouvellement composées sur plusieurs chants, tant de musique que rustique* (Paris, 1548):

> Or combien est heureuse la peine de celuy:
> Dune femme amoureuse / qui deux cueurs faict brusler
> Quant chascun deulx sentend destre content
>
> On ma dit que de lyesse mon aperan desir
> Affin quil luy plaise vn autre amy choisir:
> Mais cest abusion a toute fraction.
>
> Si mon feu sans fumee est euident et chault:
> Estant de vous aymee: destre aultre il ne men chault
> Cest le mal seul de tous / et procede de vous
>
> Il ne men chault que sois auec prince ou roy
> Mais que tousiours vous voye sans eslongner de moy
> La paour du changement: my cause vn tel tourment
>
> Si femme a ma presence autre que vous nentretiens:
> Amour veult que iaye peine: car cela mapartiens
> Il y a longue fois que estes promis a moy
>
> Vous semble il que la veue soit assees entre amys /
> Que ne ma ton proueu de ce que mest permis?
> Cest trop peu que des yeulx / amour demande mieulx
>
> A vous seule qui auez la le cueur
> Si iestois grand prince ien dirois tout ainsi:
> Si le vostre est ainsi monstrez luy par effait.
>
> (sig. D6^{r-v})

From *Le Recueil de toutes les sortes de chansons nouvelles, rustiques et musicales, et aussi ceulx qui sont dans la déploration de Vénus* (Lyon, 1555):

> Or combien est heureuse la peine de celer
> D'vne femme amoureuse, qui deux cœurs faict brusler.
> Quant chascun d'eulx s'entend d'estre content.
> On m'a dit que de liesse mon operant desir
> Affin qu'il luy plaise vn autre amy choisir
> Mais c'est abusion à toute fraction.

Si mon feu sans fumée est euident & chault
Estant de vous aimée, d'estre autre il ne m'en chault
C'est le mal seul de tous, & procede de vous.
Il ne m'en chault que sois auec prince ou Roy
Mais que tousiours vous voye sans eslongné de moy
La peur du changement, m'y cause vn tel tourment
Si femme à ma presence, autre que vous n'entretiens.
Amour veult que i'aye peine, car celà m'appartient
Il y a longue fois que estes promis à moy.
Vous semble il que la veue soit assés entre amis,
Que ne m'a on prouueu de ce qui m'est permis
C'est trop peu que des yeulx, amour demande mieulx.
A vous seule qui auez là le cueur
Si i'estois grand prince i'en dirois tout ainsi
Si le vostre est ainsi monstrez luy par effet.

(sig. c4ᵛ-c5ᵛ)

C. Latin Translations of Pseudo-Theocritus' Idyll on Adonis

Theocriti syracusani idyllia triginta-sex, Haganoæ, 1530.	*Theocriti syracusani poetæ clarissimi idyllia trigintasex*, Venice, 1539.
Adoniden Cytharea	Adonin Venus
Vt uidit interemptum	Postquàm vidit mortuum iam,
Nuperáque purpurantes	Tristem habentem cæsariem,
Genas colore fœdum	Pallidamáque genam:
Et illitum cruore	Ducere porcum ad ipsam
Nigerrino capillum	Iussit amores.
Cupidines uocauit	Hi autem statim volantes,
Et iussit ut uocati	Omnem currentes syluam,
Suem ferum sibi ipsi	Tristem porcum inuenerunt:
Adducerent præhensum	Ligaueruntáque & religauerunt.
Qui iussa prosequentes	Et hic quidem laqueo tangens,
Mox lustra peruolarunt	Trahebat captiuum;
Horrentis alta syluæ	Ille autem a tergo impellens,
Tristemáque & imbecillem	Verberabat arcubus.
Suem graue ligarunt	Fera autem ibat timide,
Rigore uinculorum	Timebat enim Venerem.
Alius trahebat autem	Huic autem dixit Venus.

Laqueo truci reuinctum
Hic terga uerberabat
Et arcubusque & ipsum
Vrentibus sagittis
Et ibat ille tristis
Veneris quidem timebat
Superba iussa duræ
Cui dixit ipsa postquàm
Conspexit esse captum
Quid pessima ò ferarum
Tu ne hoc femur decorum
Meum ne tu puellum
Insana uulnerasti?
Cui sic recepit ille
Te diua Cypris ipsum
Per & tuum puellum
Per hæc & ipsa iuro
Quæ uincla me coarctant
Item per hos amores
Qui me tulere captum
Læsisse non uolebam
Quem nunc doles puellum
Iniqua fata passum
Sed ut decora uidi
Labra & uultus honesti
Pulcherrimum nitorem
Statuam ratus deorum
Fuisse perpolitam
Flammæ nocentis hausi
Quo subruebar ignem
Quem non ferens ut illi
Nudum femur uolebam
Insanus osculari
Illi sed innocenti
Miser & mihi nocebam
Hos nunc Venus prophanos
Puni recide dentes
Superfluas, quid autem
Fero amplius, sed hæc si
Satis ampla pœna non est
Et ipsa labra puni
Hæc, illius querentis

Omnium pessima ferarum,
Tu hoc crus læsisti?
Tu mei virum verberasti?
Fera autem dixit sic.
Iuro tibi Venus,
Ipsam te, & uirum,
Et hæc mei vincula,
Et hos venatores,
Virum pulchrum tui
Non volebam percutere;
Sed tanquàm imaginem inspicie-
                              [bam
Et non ferens calorem,
Nudum habebat crus.
Insaniui osculari.
Et me concutiebat.
Hos capiens Venus,
Hos puni, incide.
Quid enim porto superfluos
Amatorios dentes.
Si autem non tibi hæc sufficiunt,
Et hæc mei labra.
Hunc autem miserata est Venus.
Dixitque amoribus,
Vincula eius soluere.
Ex hoc insequebatur,
Et syluam non ibat:
Etque igni accedens
Vrebat amores.

(ff. 58v-59r)

Venus miserta iussit
Amoribus proteruis
Vt uincla dura soluant
Et liberent ligatum
Qui mitis inde syluam
Nunquam subiunt altam
Sed ignibus propinquans
Suum nocentem amorem
Incendit & perussit.
      (sig. L1ᵛ-L2ᵛ)

D. "Adonis Theocriti ex Mellini Sangelasii Cantilena"

Quae Diua Cyprum quǽque Paphum tenet
   Postquam interemptum uidit Adonidem,
   Malásque nuper purpurantes
   Vulneribus saniéque fœdas:
Adse uocauit mœsta Cupidines,
   Et questa multum iussit ut ilico
   Adducerent ad se prehensum
   Qui puerum laniarat, aprum.
Illi exequentes iussa fideliter
   Mox peruolarunt lustra recondita,
   Syluǽque frondentis latebras,
   Atque suem tenuere sæuum.
Iniecta cui sunt stuppea uincula.
   Duro at reuincit hic laqueo trucem,
   Hic terga costasǵue illigato
   Dedolat, hic sua tela uibrat.
At ille tristis conscius & sui
   Furoris ibat permetuens Deam,
   Iras & accensas minacis,
   Propter amasiolum peremptum.
Hunc Diua captum stare ubi conspicit,
   Infit, ferarum ô pessima quid (malum?)
   Pulchrum quid inuadens Adonin
   Dente fero modò sauciasti?
En ille ceu flos uomere ferreo
   Succisus, herba nunc uiridi super
   Pallescit extentus, suóque
   Tingit humum roseo cruore.

Non te mouebat purpureus decor
   Formosi ephebi, non niueum femur,
    Et qui per albentes uolabant
    Auricomi scapulas capilli?
O biecta dein sus crimina diluit
   Vultu inferoci uoceǵue supplice,
    Per, Diua, te iuro Deosǵue
    Aethere qui numerantur, omnes:
Et per tuorum tela Cupidinum
   Formidolosa immenso etiam Ioui,
    Per, quæ ligatum me coarctant,
    Implicitis fera uincla nodis:
Me noluisse hunc lædere Adonidem,
   Nunc cuius ergò sic Dea tangeris,
    Ob fata crudeleisǵue plagas
    Queis roseus puer est necatus:
Illius ast ut labra coralina
   Vultumǵue uidi floridulum, ratus
    Vnum esse natorum tuorum, aut
    Te potius Citheræa, flammas
Hausi nocentes protinus, & femur
   Nudum ut uolebam tangere gestiens,
    Vercors & effrenis puellum
    Dente auido immeritum peremi.
Verùm innocenti dum noceo miser,
   Cultro, quod aiunt, me iugulo meo,
    Hos, Diua, quocirca prophanos
    Plecte superuacuosǵue dentes.
Vindicta quòd si non ea sufficit,
   Atque ampla non fortè est satis, ilicet
    Pœna irrogetur talionis,
    Morte luam ut parili quod actum est.
His mota demum questubus est Venus,
   Et dura iussit uincla resoluier,
    Vt liber in syluas abiret,
    Frondiferos nemorumǵue colles.
Vti data is sed non uenia tulit,
   Exactor at trux flagitii sui
    Flammis propinquauit, ruitǵue
    In medios moriturus ignes.

Chapter III

"UNE BELLE GUERRE . . . CONTRE L'IGNORANCE"

1. Form

Although it is well known that Barthélemy Aneau composed a virulent response to the *Deffence*, his *Quintil Horatian* does not constitute the only document of the day that came to the aid of Saint-Gelais and his contemporaries. Guillaume Des Autels also saw fit to decry certain claims made by Du Bellay and to counter in particular Du Bellay's negative assessment of "Laissez la verde couleur":

& ne me sauroit on oster de la fantasie, que Laissez la verde couleur, & Amour auecques Psiches, quelque nom que leur donnent ceux, qui veulent bailler des titres aux œuures d'autrui, sont vrayment œuures poëtiques, *bien ornees de figures conuenantes à leur subiet*: & que plus m'y plait, en l'vne ie voy vne prosopopœe, mouuant iusques à tout l'affection de misericorde: en l'autre vne euidence, & viue representation des choses y narees: qui n'est point encor sans l'imitation de Theocrite, combien qu'il y soit surmonté.[1]

Not only does Des Autels insist upon the general worth of the poems ("sont vrayment œuures poëtiques"), but he also thrusts at the Pléiade a characterization of each poem that brings into play the very rhetorical principles so dear to the Coqueret poets: prosopopeia that sways the emotions in "Laissez la verde couleur," enargia ("viue representation") in "Amour avecques Psyches."

Des Autels's admiration for Saint-Gelais was shared by no less a personage than Jacques Peletier du Mans, who, in his 1544 translation of the Horatian *Ars poetica*, makes a very flattering reference to our poet: "Mais en ceci peut on favorizer / Alain & Mun, & qu'un pareil credit / Soit a Marot & Merlin[2] interdit?" (f. 8ᵛ). Three years later, in his *Oeuvres poétiques*, he published an epistle addressed to Saint-Gelais (ff. 101ʳ-103ʳ). In this work Peletier defends himself against "les enuieux," but knows that, because of "certains accors spirituelz" between him and Mellin, there can be no one better to whom he can complain or, for his case, "un meilleur iuge." These are strong words from a man already committed to various ideas soon to appear in the *Deffence*, from a man whose presentation of his translation of the *Odyssey* displays considerable concern for what is inherent and forceful in Homer's style[3] and whose name figures prominently in Pasquier's list of the early warriors against ignorance.

Nevertheless, literary histories of the period have generally passed over such examples of steadfast appreciation for Saint-Gelais, presenting instead a perspective on the years such as we find in Chamard's summary of Peletier du Mans's *Oeuvres poétiques* (1547): "Si le *Blason du Cueur*, si les *Epigrammes* et l'*Epître à Mellin de Saint-Gelays* dénotaient encore un disciple de Marot, le reste était d'un éclaireur de la Pléiade: des traductions de l'antique et de l'italien, douze sonnets empruntés à Pétrarque, ... un certain nombre de *vers lyriques*, où déjà s'annonçaient quelques-uns des thèmes que devait traiter la Pléiade" (*Joachim Du Bellay*, pp. 35-36).

From the vantage point of the twentieth century, we know exactly why Chamard makes the distinctions contained in this passage, but it is by no means certain that they were evident to the world of the 1540s. The period seems rather to have enjoyed moving freely among diverse languages and genres. Thus, in Macrin's *Naeniarum libri tres*, Saint-Gelais's name is evoked (via the "Cantilena") alongside a Pindaric ode in Latin by Jean Dorat and two poems in French by Du Bellay, one a translation of another Latin poem by Dorat.[4] Antoine Du Verdier relates in his *Bibliothèque*, after the name of Jean Salmon [Macrin]: "Et si a faict des Epigrammes François bien troussez à l'imitation des Grecs, que i'ay veu escrits à la main au pouuoir d'vn libraire de Poictiers" (Lyon, 1585, p. 754). Unfortunately, we have only

Du Verdier's word for the existence of these French epigrams which would signal both fresh evidence of the importance of the epigram for poets of note before the Pléiade and interest in this genre on the part of France's most accomplished imitator of Horace in neo-Latin verse.

On the degree to which old forms were acquiring new titles and old titles were being applied to works of new inspiration, we do not need to speculate. Marot tends to equate the ballade with lyric verse and offers his final examples of the genre under titles that begin with the word "Chant." "Laissez la verde couleur" appears on Du Moulin's various title pages as a "Déploration," in Saint-Gelais's *Oeuvres* of 1547 as a "Chanson Elegie," in MS B.N. n.a. fr. 1158 as a "Lamentation"—all small, but important signs that the categorizing in which Chamard indulges ill befits the moment.

In this regard, it is interesting to note that, although Laumonier once spoke of Peletier du Mans as a "poète de transition" (*Commentaire*, p. 187), he nevertheless refused to establish firm lines of demarcation between Pléiade and pre-Pléiade practices. In an attempt to counter Chamard's contention that the potential for a wide variety in stanzaic forms did not play a significant part in attracting the Pléiade to the ode, Laumonier maintains that, "loin de mettre au second plan cette variété de mètres et cette liberté de rythmes qui pour Sebillet étaient un caractère essentiel de l'Ode, les poètes de la Pléiade leur ont accordé une importance de premier ordre, et ce faisant, *ils ont continué l'œuvre de leurs prédécesseurs*" (*Ronsard*, p. xlii, my emphasis). This statement follows closely an earlier assertion by Laumonier to the effect that the Pléiade rejected the medieval *formes fixes* in order to gain from the ode greater freedom of expression: "C'est . . . cette diversité, c'est cette liberté qui les ont séduits, au point de leur faire préférer l'Ode à toute autre forme lyrique et rejeter avec un suprême dédain le rondeau et la ballade, dont les plus graves défauts étaient à leurs yeux l'uniformité, la contrainte, la rigidité rythmiques" (p. xxxvii). Putting the two observations side by side, how can we escape the conclusion that the poets of the 1540s, too, must have recognized the superiority of the newer forms over the *formes fixes*, since, as Sébillet correctly observed, the movement away from the *formes fixes* occurred well before 1549?

Quite instructive here are lines written by Gracien Du Pont in his 1539 treatise on the subject of the chanson. So often content to repeat the views of his predecessor Pierre Fabri, Du Pont disagrees forcefully with the master on this genre. After citing a statement by Fabri which we have already quoted ("combien que Ballades & Rondeaulx . . . se mettent en chant, ne sont dictes chansons"), Du Pont speaks his own mind: "Sil entend que chanson se doibue faire tousiours de telle taille & stille, il entendroyt mal" (f. xxxviii^v). Musicians do set rondeaux and ballades to music, but "Cest au plaisir des Musiciens qui composent lesdictz chantz. Et ne sont poinct contrainctz faire lesdictz chantz sur lesdictz stilles, ains de toutes aultres formes & mesures quilz sceussent trouuer" (ff. xxxviii^v-xxxix^r). To such freedom of choice corresponds freedom of form: "Et notez que ne voyez gueres de chansons qui se ressemblent de stille & mesure" (f. xxxix^r). As a result, there can be no exhaustive definition of the chanson, and with just such an observation Du Pont closes his ruminations on the genre: "Bref ledict Fabri ny aultre nen scauroyent bailler regles suffisantes particulieres" (f. xxxix^r). Thus, almost a full decade before Sébillet wrote his *Art poétique*, a fellow theoretician had recognized the growing distinction between chanson and *formes fixes* and affirmed the association of the chanson with the broadest possible variation in form.

To be sure, the decade preceding publication of the *Deffence* exhibits a distinct fascination with the epigram, a non-stanzaic form, but, as we shall soon see, evidence for a sustained interest in stanzaic poetry is not lacking, especially if, like Ronsard and other poets of the day, we include Latin literature among the primary sources of poetic inspiration.

Beginning in 1493, an Italian, Niccolo Perotti, produced a detailed analysis of the various Horatian meters. The reception of his volume in France suggests that the forms, as well as the poems, of Horace intrigued the French. The Paris presses of Simon de Colines published the Perotti treatise in tandem with Horace's poems in 1528, 1533 and 1539 under the title of *Q. Horatii Flacci Odarum sive carminum libri quatuor*. The leap from theory to practice came with Salmon Macrin's *Carminum libri quatuor* (1530) and *Odarum libri tres* (1546). In both volumes Macrin imitates Horace's favorite strophic forms, three of which (the Sapphic Strophe, Third Asclepiad and Alcaic) contain four-line heterometric stanzas. French consciousness of these forms is further underscored in the expanded edition of Bourbon's *Nugae* (1538). There several poems bear the title "ode Sapphica," including one written to Salmon Macrin (p. 452).

This development did not take place outside the scope of vernacular literature. Ronsard reminds us of that fact when, in his introduction to the 1550 edition of the *Odes*, he describes the origin of his interest in the ode: "i'allai uoir les étrangers, & me rendi familier d'Horace, contrefaisant sa naiue douceur, des le mémc tens que Clement Marot (seulle lumiere en ses ans de la uulgaire poësie) trauailloit à la poursuite de son Psautier" (sig. A2ᵛ). Yet, even before the young Ronsard admitted to an appreciation of both Marot and Horace when learning about the lyric mode, even before publication of the "Cantilena," references to Saint-Gelais were signaling an awareness among the poets writing in French and Latin of their respective activities.

In his *Carminum libri quatuor* (1530), Salmon Macrin addresses two poems to Saint-Gelais. They tell us very little that is specific about Saint-Gelais, except to suggest that Mellin was then writing poetry for a woman named "Laodice" (f. 45ʳ). The poems assure us, however, that Saint-Gelais knew well a master of Horatian forms and that to the master the phrase "we poets" included Mellin. "Vates quietem pacis & ocia / Desideramus," writes Macrin in one of the two poems addressed to the man who will soon write the "Déploration" (f. 31ʳ).

Macrin also knew Marot and, more to the point, seems to have taken into account Marot's efforts with the psalm when experimenting himself with lyric forms. On pp. 73-75 of the *Odarum libri tres*, Salmon Macrin published a version of David's famous psalm 137 ("Super flumina Babylonis"). In the Vulgate, this psalm consists of only sixteen lines. Faithful to the Horatian cast of the *Odarum libri tres*, Salmon Macrin imposes upon the psalm the form of the Sapphic Strophe. The adaptation contains eleven quatrains, or 44 lines. The amount of added material is, thus, considerable, much greater than the comparable development we find in Marot's translation (accomplished in thirty lines). However, a comparison of the versions by the two Frenchmen reveals enough similarity to permit the conclusion that Salmon Macrin may well have consulted Marot's work when preparing his own poem. The textual similarities run as follows:

Vulgate
Quomodo cantabimus canticum Domini in terra aliena?
Marot
Las, dismes-nous, qui pourroit inciter
Nos tristes cœurs à chanter la louange
De nostre Dieu en une terre estrange?
Salmon Macrin
Carmen assuetum Dominíque laudes
Quo modo externo recinemus orbe?

Vulgate
Si oblitus fuero tui, Ierusalem, oblivioni detur dextera mea.
Marot
Or toutesfois puisse oublier ma dextre
L'art de harper, avant qu'on te voye estre,
Jerusalem hors de mon souvenir.
Salmon Macrin
Si tui oblitus Solyme decora,
Si tui Sion fuero, meæ sim
Immemor dextræ, neque blanda posthac
Nablia tangam.

Vulgate
Beatus qui tenebit et allidet parvulos tuos ad petram.
Marot
Heureux celuy qui viendra arracher
Les tiens enfans de ta mamelle impure,
Pour les froisser contre la pierre dure.
Salmon Macrin
Ille erit fœlix tibi qui reprendet
Quæ patras, quíque ad lapides rotabit
Flentium matrum pueros, ab ipso
Vbere raptos.[5]

In each instance, Macrin recalls Marot when expanding upon the biblical text. Where the Vulgate refers only to a "canticum Domini," Marot speaks of singing "la louange / De nostre Dieu," the very phrase ("Dominíque laudes") paired with "Carmen assuetum" in the neo-Latin poem to render the same verse. Marot's insertion of "L'art de harper" becomes in Salmon Macrin "blanda posthac / Nablia tangam." The image in the French psalm of children torn from their mother's impure breast, too, has no equivalent in the Vulgate text, yet it is used by Salmon Macrin, perhaps through the further influence of Virgil.[6]

Other aspects of Macrin's translation can be shown to have only classical counterparts. In the first stanza Macrin renders the verb "flevimus" with an image used by Ovid's Medea when writing to Jason of her emotion upon seeing their children: "Et, quoties video, lumina nostra madent" (*Heroides*, 12, 190). The final line of stanza three, "Compede uinctos," recalls a passage from Horace's *carmina* in which the poet tells Phyllis how her beloved Telepus has been snared by another: "tenetque grata / Compede vinctum" (VI, 11, 23-24).

The contrast in setting between these classical texts and psalm 137 is, of course, very great, yet there is every reason to believe that to Macrin the borrowed phrases were no longer associated with any particular poem, but rather with the storehouse, the "copia," of the Latin language on which future writers might draw for inspiration, an attitude by no means novel within the circle of neo-Latin writers.

In Germanus Brixius' poem *Herveus* (1513), which tells of a contemporary battle between English and French ships, the author recreates a speech by the French captain to his sailors at the moment of their impending death. References to Olympus, ambrosia and the eventual contemplation of Jupiter are mixed with the notion of purification by fire and water and of a reenactment of the martyrdom of St. Lawrence (vv. 169-97). Even closer in time and context to Macrin's efforts are various Latin paraphrases of the psalms added by Nicolas Bourbon to the 1538 edition of his *Nugae*. In his paraphrase of psalm 15 we find for "Domine quis habitabit in tabernaculo tuo? aut quis requiescet in monte sancto tuo," "O Deus, in summo quis tecum habitabit Olympo?" (p. 356). For the first verse of psalm 113, "Laudate pueri Dominum: laudate nomen Domini," Bourbon offers "Ò serui Domini, Dominum laudate tonantem" (p. 361). The association of Olympus with God's "holy mountain" and the use of the adjective "tonans" (a Jovian surname) to describe the Lord form interesting contrasts with the phrases penned by Marot to render the same verses:

> Qui est-ce qui conversera,
> O Seigneur, en ton tabernacle?
> Et qui est celuy qui sera
> Si heureux que par grace aura
> Sur ton sainct mont seur habitable?
>   (ed. Lenselink, p. 123)

> Enfans qui le Seigneur servez,
> Louez-le & son nom eslevez:
> Louez son nom & sa hautesse:
> Soit presché, soit fait solennel,
> Le nom du Seigneur eternel,
> Par tout en ce temps & sans cesse.
>   (ed. Lenselink, p. 195)

It has been claimed that Marot's psalms "contiennent l'essentiel, tout l'essentiel de la lyrique moderne."[7] However, erudition such as the Pléiade demanded for the ode clearly does not comprise part of Marot's experiment. But no matter. In a period that moved back and forth with ease between vernacular and classical literature, the psalm appears to have been a point at which converged varieties of lyric style (both simple and erudite) and form (both Marotique and Horatian, each strophic in nature), while, as Bourbon's *Nugae* reveals, ever increased interaction among poets writing in French and Latin took place. The 1533 edition of the *Nugae* contains several translations from Greek into Latin, but only one translation from a vernacular language into Latin: "Ex Franc. Petrarcha" (sig. m5ᵛ), a Latin version of "Pace non trovo." In 1538 three Latin versions of poems by Marot, as well as several pieces addressed to Marot, are added to the translations from Greek works.

Of Marot's psalms Peletier du Mans was to write in his *Art poétique* of 1555 that they fully deserved to be called odes—"ce sont vrees Odes, sinon qu'il leur defalhoet le nom, comme aus autres la chose" (ed. Boulanger, p. 176)—a declaration which implies that Peletier equated the ode with strophic structure.[8] And, in fact, when Peletier undertook to translate an epigram of Martial (to be included in his *Oeuvres poétiques* with translations from Petrarch and Horace), Martial's non-stanzaic work of thirteen lines becomes in the resulting French a typical example of the new lyric form: six octosyllabic quatrains with the same rhyme scheme in each, but with new rhymes for each quatrain. Moreover, no ode in *rimes plates* appears in Peletier's *Oeuvres*, where, when translating Horace, the poet gives the impression of having attempted in the main to find suitable stanzaic equivalents for the *carmina* in question.[9] The Sapphic Strophe of "Otium divos" is rendered by quatrains of three alexandrins plus one six-syllable verse, that is, by a quatrain that matches the Latin meter in length, save for one syllable added per line. Each stanza is not entirely independent, however, as the last line of every even-numbered quatrain rhymes with the last line of the preceding quatrain, a form reminiscent of one of Scève's two translations from the psalms.[10] A version of psalm 126, the poem proceeds in units of three verses in which the last line of stanzas 2, 4, 6, etc., rhymes with the final verse of the preceding stanza (aab ccb dde ffe, and so forth).

Horace's "Quid dedicatum," composed in his favorite strophe, the Alcaic, Peletier rendered by huitains of six-syllable lines. Thus, an isometric stanza replaces the near-uniformity of the four Latin lines of 11, 11, 9 and 10 syllables respectively. "Beatus ille," a work in Iambic Strophes, that is, alternating verses of 12 and 8 syllables, undergoes severe transformation. Peletier's version is couched in isometric sizains of octosyllabic verse. The rhyme scheme, aabccb, is the same used by Marot in his translations of psalms 6, 24, 38, 103, 113, 114, 115 (two of which are also in octosyllabic verse), a form that breaks utterly with the medieval sizain, constructed on two rhymes.

Marot's influence extends to the poems Peletier published under the heading of "Vers lyriques." "A un poete qui n'escriuoit qu'en Latin" corresponds to the schema of psalm 10 (a seven-line stanza rhymed ababbcc), with the exception that Peletier uses octosyllabic verse and Marot decasyllabic verse.

The schema of "A ceulx qui blament les Mathematiques," quatrains rhymed abab of alternating octosyllabic and six-syllable lines, recalls the quatrains of psalms 72 and 91;[11] "A un sien amy" (sizains rhymed aabccb with a and c composed of octosyllabic lines and b of six-syllable lines) reproduces the schema of psalm 36.

Of such poetic activity the *Deffence* does not speak. Instead, its denunciation of the (unnamed) "ambicieux admirateurs des Langues Grecque & Latine" (ed. Chamard, p. 28) implies, and literary history has tended to agree, that the efforts of these writers mean little with respect to the development of French poetry. Yet surely this is not true, if only in the sense that Salmon Macrin and others reinforce and expand upon the scope of an on-going experimentation with lyric forms. Interaction between the French and Latin tongues was not foreign even to the Pléiade. The 1555 printing of Ronsard's *Hinne de Bacus* contains a Latin translation of the French by Dorat on the facing pages. The invitation to compare and contrast could not be more blatant. If we knew today in what spirit this volume was offered and read, we would possess an invaluable insight into a practice that has long remained unappreciated.

When Alexandre Machard reproduced in 1879 the text of the first printing of Théodore de Bèze's *Poemata*, he saw fit to translate only the epigrams and epitaphs. The "Silves" he considered mere "exercices de Rhétorique," the "Elegiae," "une reproduction facile des formes élégiaques Latines" (p. viii). It is doubtful that the *Deffence* can be blamed for Machard's disparaging attitude towards rhetoric and facile reproduction of Latin forms; nevertheless, by dismissing the neo-Latins and most vernacular poetry, the treatise cannot be said to have encouraged us to view in a positive light the presence in French literary circles, through neo-Latin poetry, of classical forms and language, even though it is not impossible that Pasquier, when including Bèze among the "auant-coureurs," had in mind the very portions of the *Poemata* that Machard declined to translate into modern French.[12] What is certain is that Pasquier singled out the three "auant-coureurs" for their common desire to "plus contenter leurs esprits, que l'opinion du commun peuple" (p. 615). This trait may help explain the absence of Saint-Gelais from Pasquier's list. The public Saint-Gelais sought to please delighted most often in the superficial, not the elevated tonalities of lyric verse. Yet throughout this chapter we have also seen our poet at the crossroads of serious experimentation with form and language. If Saint-Gelais is not a harbinger of the Pléiade, is he at least an impressive soldier in the campaign to move beyond the once-dominant *formes fixes*? Again, "Laissez la verde couleur" can help us in our search for a surer judgment.

2. "Translation ou allusion"

In the preceding discussion a number of titles have been cited which point to the desire of French poets in the 1540s to render pre-existing verse into another language. We have seen that Peletier translates Petrarch, Martial and Horace into French and that a Greek poem by Pseudo-Theocritus is translated into Latin. The list could be expanded to include one of the pieces Du Bellay contributed to the *Naeniarum libri tres* ("Imitation de l'ode latine de Iehan Dorat sur la mort de la Roine de Navarre") and translations into Latin by Nicolas Bourbon of the work of Marot and Petrarch. Although Du Bellay will speak negatively about translations in the *Deffence*, the signs are strong that the war against ignorance pursued during the 1540s included exercises in language as well as form and that the practice of reproducing a text in another tongue brought with it no disgrace. Consider, for example, the fact that the 1547 edition of Saint-Gelais's works bore as its full title: *Saingelais, Oeuvres de luy, tant en composition que translation, ou allusion aux auteurs grecs et latins*. Indeed, long before Ronsard takes up the story of Adonis as told by Ovid and weaves into his retelling of the myth clear echoes of Navagero and Bion,[13] Saint-Gelais may be said to have attempted a similar feat in "Laissez la verde couleur."

Saint-Gelais's debt to Bion has long been recognized, even over-emphasized. The notes to the Blanchemain edition of the poem presuppose that the poet wrote "Laissez la verde couleur" with Bion's work before him. This assumption encountered more than one problem, however. "Je ne puis deviner pourquoi," writes one of the editors, "ayant sous les yeux le πορ ψυρέοις ψάρεσι du poëte grec, il a substitué le verd au rouge" (I, 133). Later the same editor expresses surprise at Saint-Gelais's verse "O demeure du Ciel tiers": "Nous devons la connoissance de ce troisième ciel à saint Paul, qui dit y avoir été ravi, et il est assez particulier que Sainct-Gelays fasse parler à Vénus le langage de saint Paul" (I, 135).

In a 1944 article Saulnier identified the presence of the phrase "verde couleur" in Saint-Gelais's poem as a borrowing from the tenth eglogue of Luigi Alamanni: "Lascia ó Venere bella il uerde e 'l bianco" ("Etude," p. 52), thus adding Alamanni to the list of possible sources for the famous "Déploration," a list that must also include Amomo, Ovid, Pseudo-Theocritus and Virgil.[14] All these poets do, in fact, contribute to "Laissez la verde couleur," although each is not used because he sang of Adonis.

A rather faithful adaptation of Bion's Greek text, the Amomo poem ("Epitaphio di Adone di Theocrito") retains several aspects also present in Saint-Gelais, such as the comparison of Adonis' wound to that produced in Venus by love, the reference to Echo and to Proserpina, the image of Venus crying out her woes as she rushes through the vales, and the notation that the tears Venus sheds match the amount of blood lost by Adonis. Moreover, although Saint-Gelais's lines "Et de sa belle main blanche / Sa playe luy ha touchee" (vv. 19-20) have no equivalent in Bion, they recall two passages in Amomo: "Adone / Che non uede ch'il tocci" and "Come gli stende poi la bianca mano" (sig. E3r, E4r). However, the Amomo text throws no light on the question raised regarding the presence of "le Ciel tiers" in Saint-Gelais's poem. For the source of that image, we must turn again to Alamanni.

His tenth eglogue, entitled "Adone," consists of a dialogue between Daphni and Menalca, each of whom sings a portion of the Bion text. To be more precise, each sings a portion of those Greek verses Alamanni chose to translate. For example, no reference to Echo or to Venus pouring out her lament to the vales appears in Alamanni's version. All the other segments from Bion listed above as used by Saint-Gelais and translated by Amomo are equally present in "Adone," and in a form that provides no clear indication that it or the other Italian text alone may have inspired Saint-Gelais. Still, just as the case for Amomo's influence must underscore the interpolation of a statement about Venus touching Adonis with her white hand, so a case for Alamanni's influence can be built on the fact that, in addition to the verse quoted above, his translation of Bion's "même mort il est beau dans la mort, comme s'il reposait" (vs. 71) comes closer to the phrasing of "Laissez la verde couleur" when it appeared in print for the first time in 1545. Saint-Gelais divided Bion's thought between two stanzas:

> Toutesfois de mort attaint
> Il n'ha de rien empiree
> La grand' beaulté de son taint
> (vv. 33-35)

and

> Ainsi le piteux Amant
> Avoit la teste appuyee,
> Comme s'il estoit dormant.
> (vv. 41-43)

Alamanni translates the pertinent Greek passages by "morto è bello anchora / Tal che non morto anzi dormir ne sembra" (p. 158). Amomo renders the verse with "Par ch'habbia gli occhi sui dormendo chiusi / Tanto bella par morte al suo bel uolto" (sig. E5^r).

Secondly, in "Laissez la verde couleur" we find an entire quatrain devoted to the gathering of birds to sing their sorrow at Adonis' passing (vv. 61-64). Neither Bion nor Amomo even alludes to such a phenomenon. But Alamanni writes, "Piangan gli augei, le piante, i fiori, & l'herbe" (p. 156).

More conclusive yet, however, is the relationship between Alamanni's poem and the perplexing question of the "Ciel tiers." If Saint-Gelais saw no reason not to include a Pauline phrase among Venus' words, a simple explanation may be that Alamanni had already done just that. In "Adone" the first shepherd makes Venus ask, "Hor chi pensò giamai che 'l terzo cielo / Porti inuidia à colui che corre à morte" (p. 157).

Ovid's influence on the poem often appears in passages that make use of and reshape their model to a significant degree. Ovid, not Bion, makes reference to the swans that draw Venus' chariot, yet a considerable distance separates the brief "junctisque per aera cygnis / Carpit iter" (X, 708-09) from the role Saint-Gelais determined for the birds:

> Et mesmes ses deux blancz Cygnes
> Chanson piteuse ont chantee.
> Mais voyant l'obscure nuict
> Estre jà presque arrivee,
> Ont doulcement et sans bruit
> Leur maistresse en l'air levee.
> (vv. 151-56)

Similarly, Venus' apostrophe to Adonis,

> Et vous, Amy trop espris
> De vostre force esprouvee,
> Si mon conseil eussiez pris,
> Mieux je m'en fusse trouvee.
> Cerfs, Dains, et bestes fuyantes
> Estoyent mieux vostre portee
> Que les fieres et bruyantes
> Qui m'ont tant desconfortee.
> (vv. 121-28)

contains only echoes of Ovidian material:

"vostre force"	"virtus tua" (X, 707)
"Cerfs, Dains, et bestes fuyantes"	"Aut pronos lepores, aut celsum in cornua cervum, / Aut agitat dammas" (X, 538-39)
"Que les fieres et bruyantes / Qui m'ont tant desconfortee"	"Impetus est fulvis et vasta leonibus ira; / Invisumque mihi genus est" (X, 551-52)

The clearest borrowing occurs, perhaps not unexpectedly, when Saint-Gelais speaks of the flowers touched by Adonis' blood and by Venus' tears. Although the description of the actual metamorphosis derives from Bion, the quatrain

Ce taint leur demourera
Pour enseigne de duree
Tant que le monde sera
De leur grand peine enduree
(vv. 57-60)

contains an Ovidian touch: "luctus monimenta manebunt / Semper, Adoni, mei" (X, 725-26), a *rapprochement* which helps us to understand better the somewhat tortured syntax of the stanza. The sequence of ideas would appear to be "Ce taint leur demourera / Tant que le monde sera / Pour enseigne de [la] duree / De leur grand peine enduree," with the first "leur" referring to the flowers and the second to Venus and Adonis.

Although the list of identifiable influences upon Saint-Gelais for this single poem is rather long, it must also be clear from the above that the number of verses in the "Déploration" borrowed *in toto* from a classical or Italian source remains rather small. Even if one counts the lines with distant sources, only about 100 verses out of 160 have echoes elsewhere (and half of them belong to the category of quite distant echoes). "Laissez la verde couleur" evokes all the appropriate antecedents in literature dealing with Venus and Adonis without slavishly reproducing the substance of any one of them. Throughout the poem Saint-Gelais develops and extends his source material. Fully a third of the poem reflects the technique we have observed in the echoes from Amomo and Ovid. Yet another third cannot be said to derive at all from the works of Ovid or Bion or Pseudo-Theocritus or any other poet we have mentioned above.

Not every innovation proves felicitous. Perhaps because Bion's work already contained an allusion to Ceres' daughter Proserpina, the French poem follows its reworking of that allusion with reference to Proserpina's husband:

Vienne le grand ravisseur
De l'infernale contree,
Il pourra bien estre seur
D'avoir faveur rencontree.
(vv. 81-84)

Even though the quatrain is consistent with Venus' desire to share mortality with the dead Adonis and to join him in the underworld, Pluto's reputation as a "ravisseur" derives from his rapt of Proserpina to be his wife in Hades. In order to accept the image as expressed by Saint-Gelais, we must forget the motive behind Pluto's action and remember only where Proserpina was taken.

Venus' words to Juno,

> N'ayez plus sur moy d'envie,
> Royne du Ciel honoree.
> Puisqu'Adonis est sans vie,
> Peu vault ma Pomme doree
> (vv. 93-96)

present no such difficulty and convey aptly, even if by means of a well-known element of classical lore, the low estate to which the once victorious goddess has fallen.

For Blanchemain, the image that opens the poem, "Laissez la verde couleur," was to be taken figuratively, since green signifies hope. The editors were apparently not familiar with Alamanni's line, however, or with the passage where it appears. Had this been the case, they might have offered a slightly different interpretation.

Saint-Gelais's source reads, "Lascia ó Venere bella il uerde e 'l bianco, / Lascia il uermiglio, e 'n brune spoglie auuolta" (p. 155). Alamanni has expanded upon the Greek text which, too, commands Venus, but quite differently: "Ne sommeille plus, Kypris, sur ta couche de pourpre. Eveille-toi, malheureuse, prends de sombres vêtements" (vv. 3-4). Alamanni's reworking effects a firm contrast between certain bright colors and the somber shades that now befit the bereft goddess' misfortune. An entrance into mourning, not abandonment of hope, would, therefore, be a more likely reading of the verse Saint-Gelais borrowed from Alamanni. Its function in the poem need not end there, however.

It may be conjectured that Saint-Gelais read beyond the opening of Alamanni's poem. After all, farther along he found and, we assume, borrowed the reference to the "Ciel tiers." He would have found also a development of the original light/dark contrast he used in the first line of the "Déploration." For example, Bion's image "les roses fuient de sa lèvre" (vs. 11) becomes in the Italian "l'ardenti rose / Lascian le labbra che 'l pallore ingombra" (p. 155). Later "Jette sur lui des couronnes et des fleurs; que toutes avec lui, que toutes les fleurs aussi meurent, puisqu'il est mort" (vv. 75-76) is rendered by

> Quanto ha uerde il terren, quant' ha 'l ciel chiaro,
> Quanto ha 'l mar lieto, & dolce, & fresco l'acque,
> Et col tuo uago fior si perda aprile,
> Che dopo il morir suo, dopo 'l tuo pianto,
> Veder non si conuien che notte & uerno.
>
> (p. 158)

The French poem does not lack references to color as it unfolds, and those references suggest that Saint-Gelais, too, determined to use color to underscore the drama portrayed.

No sooner have we heard of the spot where Adonis "Avoit ses beaux yeux ternis / Et de sang l'herbe arrosee" (vv. 15-16), that is, no sooner does Saint-Gelais remind us of the fading of life from Adonis (repeated in the flowing of his blood upon the [green] grass), than the poet situates Venus:

> Dessoubz une verte branche
>   Aupres de luy s'est couchee,
>   Et de sa belle main blanche
>   Sa playe luy ha touchee.
>
>   (vv. 17-20)

Two colors are mentioned, both included by Alamanni among those that Venus must relinquish, one used by Saint-Gelais to open his work. Nevertheless, the colors green and white return, describing Venus' beauty and the world Adonis leaves behind. Although at the approach of death light drains from the eyes of the young shepherd, although what greenness Adonis' blood has touched is changed, and Venus, too, must show the effect of his passing in her dress, nature in general, as well as Venus' immortal loveliness, is unaltered. Thus, a poem that begins with an emphasis on change and death quickly adopts a more complicated portrait of the tragic event. The perspective of verses such as "Vostre œil plus ne le voirra" (vs. 7) gives way to juxtaposition, as in "de sang l'herbe arrosee. / Dessoubz une verte branche" and in "belle main blanche / Sa playe," preparing the reader for the fullness of Saint-Gelais's statement.

An early indication of that statement is given in vv. 21-24, a quatrain constructed around another juxtaposition:

> O nouvelle cruaulté,
> De veoir en pleurs si baignee
> La Deesse de beaulté
> D'amy mort accompaignee.
> (vv. 21-24)

The goddess of beauty, Venus of the white hand, lies beside the lifeless, colorless beloved. The underlying drama—a contrast between the mortal lover and the ever beautiful, immortal survivor—will gradually move to the surface of the poem and infuse some of the work's most poetic moments.

The comparison of a dying flower to passing beauty was already a commonplace by the beginning of the sixteenth century. In vv. 37-40, Saint-Gelais compares Adonis to a white rose touched by a "poignante ongle," but not with the intention of conveying the familiar truth about human mortality. Rather, he prepares the scene of Adonis lying against the bereaved goddess. Not death, but the plucked flower's inevitable fall, is stressed:

> Mais comme une rose blanche,
> De poignante ongle touchee,
> Ne peut tenir sur la branche,
> Mais sur une autre est couchee,
> Ainsi le piteux Amant
> Avoit la teste appuyee,
> Comme s'il estoit dormant
> Sur sa maistresse ennuyee.
> (vv. 37-44)

What could so easily have been the repetition of a tired image becomes instead a renewal of the commonplace for the purposes at hand ("Mais sur une autre est couchee") without any loss of its evocative power ("Ne peut tenir sur la branche").

The poem's close contains an amalgam of pointed borrowing (from Virgil), mere evocation of writings on Venus and Adonis and distinct originality. As night falls, Venus turns to Adonis,

> Disant, "Las, l'heure est venue
> Que toute chose créee
> De sa peine soustenue
> Dormant sera recréee."
>
>   (vv. 141-44)

Here Saint-Gelais follows the *Aeneid*: "Cetera per terras omnis animalia somno / laxabant curas et corda oblita laborum" (IX, 224-25). In the ensuing verses, the presence of Echo recalls Bion; the swans, Ovid. But they prove to be only brief reminiscences that Saint-Gelais will recast in order to give his "Déploration" an elegant and moving end, one quite unlike those we find in Ovid or Bion.

The Greek text bids Venus cease her weeping: "Tu auras à pleurer de nouveau, une autre année de nouveau tu auras à verser des larmes" (vv. 97-98). Ovid closes the story and Book X with the birth of a flower from Adonis' blood which in turn gives rise to a final observation about the brevity of the flower's life: "brevis est tamen usus in illo; / Namque male haerentem et nimia levitate caducum / Excutiunt idem, qui praestant nomina, venti" (X, 737-39). In "Laissez la verde couleur," after transcribing the Virgilian lines, Saint-Gelais uses them to heighten Venus' torment:[15]

> Mais pour moy les jours et nuictz
> N'ont point d'heure disposee
> A terminer mes ennuictz
> Et me trouver reposee.
>
>   (vv. 145-48)

To continue, yet vary, the emphasis on despair, the poet makes use of Echo and Venus' swans. Echo is described as "tourmentee" and the swans' song as "piteuse." Then come the final quatrains:

> Mais voyant l'obscure nuict
>   Estre jà presque arrivee,
>   Ont doulcement et sans bruit
>   Leur maistresse en l'air levee.
> Plus elle approche des Cieulx,
>   Plus tient la teste baissee,
>   Et eust voulentiers ses yeulx
>   Et sa veuë en bas laissee.
>   (vv. 153-60)

Whereas Saint-Gelais's classical predecessors end the event with references that extend beyond the time-frame of the Venus and Adonis story, the French poet seeks a conclusion appropriate for both tale and poem. Again juxtaposition serves his purpose.

After the drama of Adonis' death and of Venus' reaction, the swans effect a gentle, noiseless retreat. Night falls, blotting out the precise details of Adonis' beauty and blood-stained wound, details which must grow even more indistinct as Venus, and the reader, withdraw from the scene. To the central contrast between mortal lover and immortal goddess, Saint-Gelais devotes the entire final quatrain. The closer Venus comes to the heavens and her celestial abode, the more she bows her head, partly in grief, no doubt, but partly because, as the last lines reveal, she would gladly fix her gaze where her lover lies dead.

This chapter began with a comment by Guillaume Des Autels on the quality of "Laissez la verde couleur." Our own analysis would substantiate his defense of the work, but it remains to be seen whether the poetic sense exhibited by Saint-Gelais in that poem reappears elsewhere with sufficient frequency to signal beyond any doubt his participation in the "war" of Pasquier's "auant-coureurs."

"Davidis Psalmus CXXXVII"
(from J. Salmon Macrin's *Odarum libri tres*, pp. 73-75)

Barbaræ propter Babylonis amnes
   Sedimus mœsti, memorésque, Sion,
   Cum tui essemus, maducre largo
      Lumina fletu.

Amnium ripis salices uirebant
   Pendulæ, erectis per inane ramis,
   Nostra pendebant ubi cum relictis
      Barbita plectris.

Carmen instabant patrios & hymnos
   Vt sono dulci caneremus, illi
   Duxerant qui nos Babylona tristi
      Compede uinctos.

Carmen assuetum Dominíque laudes
   Quo modo externo recinemus orbe?
   Incolæ cuius simulachra adorant
      Vana Deorum?

Si tui oblitus Solyme decora,
   Si tui Sion fuero, meæ sim
   Immemor dextræ, neque blanda posthac
      Nablia tangam.

Lingua adhærescat taciturna mutis
   Faucibus, fari ualeat nec unquam,
   Præferam ni te, Solyme alma, genti
      Laudibus omni.

Fecero primam nisi te inter urbes
   Gaudio exultans alias, Sed ô qui
   Axe de summo Deus alme terras
      Despicis imas:

Esto Idumææ memor oro gentis,
   Intulit nobis mala quanta cerne,
   Nostra quàm fœdis dedit & ruinis
     Mœnia pessum.

Cum cohortatus fremitu minaci
   Inuicem sese stimularet hostis,
   Vertite inuisam, quatite háncque, clamans,
     Funditus urbem.

Tu quoque insultans nimis impotenter
   Es breui infœlix Babylon futura,
   Et reponetur tibi quicquid in nos
     Ausa fuisti.

Ille erit fœlix tibi qui rependet
   Quæ patras, quíque ad lapides rotabit
   Flentium matrum pueros, ab ipso
     Vbere raptos.

Chapter IV

IMITATION

Over the course of his career Saint-Gelais imitated works by Horace, Ovid, Catullus, Sannazaro, Navagero, Second, Petrarch, Martial, the poets of the Greek Anthology, Anacreon, Berni, Serafino and Ariosto. In several instances, the same works would soon attract the Pléiade as well, a firm sign of Saint-Gelais's poetic sense, but no less of the continuum that characterizes many features of literary history in the period before and after the *Deffence*.

It is quite possible that Saint-Gelais imitated poets whose names are not present in the list just given. Source hunting, especially in the Renaissance, is a perilous enterprise. All that has been written about Saint-Gelais's debt to the Greek Anthology, for example, cannot be supported by the texts in question.

James Hutton has said that Saint-Gelais "translates or echoes" fifteen texts from the Greek Anthology (p. 319); Molinier enumerates seven "principal" borrowings from the Anthology and four questionable cases (p. 467), not always those indicated by Hutton. By my count, only nine instances of a close bond between Saint-Gelais and the Greek poems can be noted:

Blanchemain edition	Palatine Anthology
II, 297 "Amour me fit"	5, 36
I, 110 "Ces six œillets"	5, 74
II, 57 "J'en aime deux"	5, 269
II, 90 "Point n'ay"	7, 669
II, 146 "Je ne saurois"	7, 669
III, 146 "Qui s'est sauvé"	9, 133

III, 6	"Fortune avoit"	9, 627
II, 164	"S'on ne mouroit"	11, 171
II, 8	"Toute femme"	11, 381

The association of Saint-Gelais's dizain "Si j'ay du bien, hélas! c'est par mensonge" (Blanchemain, I, 107) with Palatine Anthology 5, 237, an association made by the Blanchemain edition and by both Molinier and Hutton, definitely leads us down a false path. The dizain derives from the *Orlando Furioso*, canto 33, stanza 62, which is also the source for sonnet 28 of Du Bellay's *L'Olive*. Curiously, Vianey links that stanza and the following stanza from the *Furioso* with Saint-Gelais's dizains 35 and 36 (Blanchemain, II, 108-09), although there is no relationship at all between the French and Italian texts (*Le Pétrarquisme*, p. 52, n. 3).

Although we shall not find in these borrowings from the Greek Anthology further evidence of Saint-Gelais's capacity "de plus contenter [son esprit], que l'opinion du commun peuple," the poems are useful to us from several points of view. As mentioned above, they lend substance to the possibility that Saint-Gelais knew Greek well enough to translate Bion when he was composing "Laissez la verde couleur." Since we find Du Bellay following Saint-Gelais's lead in at least one instance, the influence of the Greek Anthology underscores also the persistent enjoyment of light and mannered poetry beyond the 1540s, whatever thrust the *Deffence* gives to more learned verse.[1] Finally, even in this context of superficial badinage, comparisons can be made between Saint-Gelais and the Pléiade to show the varying degrees of skill with which Mellin could compete in the exacting art of imitation.

The douzain "Ces six œillets" (Blanchemain, I, 110)[2] and Ronsard's "Je vous envoye un bouquet" (*Oeuvres complètes*, VII, 152-53) both bear a close resemblance to an epigram from the Greek Anthology in which the gift of a crown of flowers is meant to remind the beloved of her mortality (5, 74). In his poem Saint-Gelais begins by explaining the symbolism of the flowers' colors. The gray blooms recall his pain; the red ones, the fact that the God of love draws blood from him for sustinence. Then the poet reveals the overall message: beauty is ephemeral; "qui l'ha la doit mettre en usage." Although the symbolism of the flowers does not appear in the original Greek, its addition to the substance of the epigram cannot surprise us, given the period's interest in the significance of colors,[3] but if we compare Saint-Gelais's poem with Ronsard's sonnet, we observe in the way the douzain develops such symbolism all the terseness of the epigrammatic style at its most unappealing, whereas in the latter piece the poet treats his material with intense vividness.

The flowers, writes Saint-Gelais,

> . . . ayans de leur nature
> Breve saison, vous portent ce message
> Que la beauté est un bien qui peu dure,
> Et que qui l'ha la doit mettre en usage.

Not only is the message dispatched without emphasis, but also its implication for the couple receives but an oblique allusion. Ronsard chooses to underscore immediately the fragility of the flowers: "Qui ne les eust à ce vespre cuillies, / Flaques à terre elles cherroient demain." This permits direct reference in the second quatrain to the inevitable passing of the lady's "beautés," a reference intensified by the strategic placement of the adverb "suddenly": "Et periront, comme ces fleurs, soudain." The tercets open with "Le tems s'en va, le tems s'en va, ma Dame." Then the poet quickly corrects himself. Not time, but we pass: "Las! le tems non, mais nous nous en allons, / Et tost serons estendus sous la lame." Indeed, in counterdistinction to the douzain, drama pervades the sonnet, first through the suddenness with which the truth may become manifest and then through the rhetorical *revirement* of "Las! le tems non, mais nous nous en allons" and the painful contrast of the poem's conclusion: "Et des amours desquelles nous parlons, / Quand serons morts n'en sera plus nouvelle." Here the palm clearly goes to Ronsard, but Saint-Gelais's sense of the requirements for a successful epigram did not fail him when he reworked Second's seventh basium.[4]

From Second's 34 lines Saint-Gelais fashioned this dizain:

Cent mille foys & en cent mille sortes
Ie baiserois ceste bouche & ces yeux,
Lors que mes mains plus que les vostres fortes
Vous rendent prise, & moy victorieux:
Mais, en baisant, mon oeil trop curieux
De voir le bien que ma bouche luy cache
Se tire arriere, & seul à ioüir tasche
De la beauté qu'il perd quand il y touche[.]
Deuinez doncq' s'vn autre amy me fasche
Puys que mon oeil est ialoux de ma bouche.[5]

Second helped the French poet to condense the Latin work by twice elaborating upon peripheral aspects of the central theme. Second begins his poem with an eleven-line segment devoted to hortatory thoughts on the number of kisses he would like to plant upon his beloved. Later he compares the capacity of her smiles to drive away his cares to Apollo scattering the clouds and moving quickly through the air in his chariot. The first passage Saint-Gelais reduces to the initial lines of the dizain; the second he omits entirely. Should we attach any importance to this omission, especially since the Latin passage contains the kind of mythological embellishment that Ronsard will soon employ in so many poems? Is Saint-Gelais's preference for the compact dizain an indication of at least part of the distance that separates literary tastes of the 1540s from the Pléiade esthetic?

The reference made in "Laissez la verde couleur" to Pluto and Juno, where Saint-Gelais's sources neither contained nor hinted at such allusions, assure us that Saint-Gelais did not eschew the use of mythology. But "Laissez la verde couleur" is not an epigram, and that distinction may provide some insight into the poet's thinking.

The diction of "Laissez la verde couleur" suggests that, unlike various poets of the day of the Reform persuasion, Saint-Gelais did not feel uncomfortable singing of profane love or using, as Théodore de Bèze phrases it in the introduction to *Abraham Sacrifiant*, "manieres de parler trop eslongnées du commun." The omission in "Cent mille foys" would, thus, seem to point rather to an association in Saint-Gelais's mind between epigram and "un langage naïf, naturel, et sans fard, net et familier," to borrow Guillaume Colletet's description of the epigrammatic style.[6] Certainly the effort expended in the dizain moves toward a sustained exploitation of the theme of rivalry between eyes and lips that is present in, yet diffused throughout, the basium. Lines 3 and 4 of the dizain, for example, have no clear equivalent in the Latin text. They establish at the outset a position of strength and superiority for the lover which will then be contrasted with the trials experienced by his eyes and the hint of anger before any rival. The pivotal point in the poem is marked by the conjunction "Mais," which introduces the very opposite portrait of "moy victorieux." The eye only "à ioüir tasche / De la beauté qu'il perd," and the lover rounds out his statement with reference to annoyance and jealousy. Here (and distinctly *not* because this is an imitation) we find no trace of the epigram Du Bellay dismissed as having nothing to say, save "le petit mot pour rire" in the final line.

This judgment by Du Bellay proves all the more interesting when we consider his own adaptation of canto 33, stanza 62 of the *Orlando Furioso*, a passage that also inspired Saint-Gelais:

Ariosto

Fu quel che piacque, un falso sogno; e questo
che mi tormenta, ahi lassa! è un veggiar vero.
Il ben fu sogno a dileguarsi presto,
ma non è sogno il martìre aspro e fiero.
Perch'or non ode e vede il senso desto
quel ch'udire e veder parve al pensiero?
A che condizione, occhi miei, sète,
che chiusi il ben, e aperti il mal vedete?

Du Bellay's adaptation

Ce que je sen', la langue ne refuse
Vous decouvrir, quand suis de vous absent,
Mais tout soudain que près de moy vous sent,
Elle devient et muette et confuse.

Ainsi, l'espoir me promect et m'abuse:
Moins près je suis, quand plus je suis present:
Ce qui me nuist, c'est ce qui m'est plaisent:
Je quier' cela, que trouver je recuse.

Joyeux la nuit, le jour triste je suis:
J'ay en dormant ce qu'en veillant poursuis:
Mon bien est faulx, mon mal est veritable.

D'une me plain', et deffault n'est en elle.
Fay' doncq', Amour, pour m'estre charitable,
Breve ma vie ou ma nuit eternelle.

                              (*L'Olive*, XXVIII)

Stanza 62 is constructed upon a set of contrasts: joy comes from a dream, that is, from something false; what is true produces torment. In adapting this material, Du Bellay deals freely with Ariosto, adding to the content of stanza 62 some elements of stanza 63 (notably in the second quatrain and second tercet) and creating an introductory quatrain to prepare his development of the basic contrasts. Saint-Gelais, as we shall see, remains much closer to his source. Yet both respond to the antitheses contained in the *Furioso* passage and even accentuate them when, for instance, in the first quatrain Du Bellay contrasts presence and absence and the resulting ability or inability of the poet's tongue to speak his feelings, all features added to the Italian material.

The subsequent movement into Ariosto's verses occurs with some awkwardness. Line 5, "Ainsi l'espoir me promect et m'abuse," incorporates a verb used in the opening of stanza 63 ("Il dolce sonno mi promise pace"), a borrowing that aids us considerably in grasping Du Bellay's elliptical thought. "L'espoir," it would seem, refers to the substance of the poet's dream, which is full of promise, yet false. Still, such information is of limited help in deciphering the remainder of the second quatrain.

The first word of the second quatrain, "Ainsi," can be variously interpreted. It may imply a conclusion ("Thus") in the light of what has preceded; it may be part of an elliptical comparison: "[Just as] my tongue does not refuse to disclose what I feel when absent from you, yet near you becomes mute, so . . . ." Whichever meaning was intended, the fact remains that "Ainsi" obliges the reader to seek out a relationship between the two quatrains, yet neither meaning can be used to establish a coherent link between the segments of the sonnet.

As regards a possible comparison, there is no qualitative similarity between volubility and promise, silence and deception;
secondly, the actions described in each case are not comparable.
To be sure, the content of line 6—to be farther, the closer he is—
makes some sense if we remember that "hope" is synonymous
with "dream." The closer the poet is to his lady, the farther
he is in fact from the intimacy suggested by his dreams. Also,
tongue and hope do have in common two contrasting functions,
but line 6 states the contrast in terms of simultaneous action
("me promect et m'abuse"), whereas the schema of the first
quatrain is based on different responses to different situations
("quand . . . / Mais . . . que").

The second possibility contained in "Ainsi" proves no less
difficult to develop. If, as a result of the situation described
in the first quatrain, "l'espoir [l]e promect et [l]'abuse," the
absence in the first quatrain of all three terms from this phrase
—hope, promise, deception—or even related concepts makes it
hard to follow Du Bellay's reasoning.

Lines 7 and 8 are more puzzling still, particularly in comparison with Du Bellay's source. The opening verses of stanza 62
from the *Furioso* contrast being asleep and being awake, pleasure and torment. Du Bellay writes, "Ce qui me nuist, c'est ce
qui m'est plaisent," placing pleasure and torment in the same
phenomenon. Is the poet expanding upon the idea that "l'espoir" both promises (gives pleasure) and deceives (hurts)? It is
possible, but the result recalls the asymmetry discussed with
regard to line 6. The tongue is not both voluable and mute at
the same time, but one or the other, depending on whether the
poet's lady is present or absent. Interestingly enough, not until
Du Bellay composed the first tercet did he use the double set
of contrasts that is sketched by Ariosto (night vs. day, happy
vs. sad) and mimicked in the first quatrain (presence vs. absence,
volubility vs. silence).

The statement "Je quier' cela que trouver je recuse" must
be the most difficult of all to explain. Quoting this very line,
Huguet glosses "recuser" with "refuser de," but the translation
clarifies little. The contrast between seeking and refusing to find
has no equivalent in Ariosto, no preparation in what precedes

in Du Bellay's sonnet, and no explanation in what follows. Is "recuser" perhaps a Latinism, appearing here as the verb *recuso* is used by Virgil in the *Aeneid*, 2,126 and 2,607 with the meaning (recorded in Lewis and Short) of "be reluctant or unwilling to do a thing"? With this interpretation of "recuser" Du Bellay would be stating that what he seeks he is reluctant to find, since, as the first quatrain tells us, to be close to the lady is to experience confusion. Moreover, actual proximity to the woman only accentuates the distance between them ("moins près je suis, quand plus je suis present"). Such a reading of "recuser" can be only an hypothesis, and the extent to which we must reach beyond the literal givens of the text in order to render them comprehensible underscores anew the problematic nature of the sonnet. We can be sure of only one thing: Du Bellay wished to transform Ariosto's stanza into an even more extravagant accumulation of antitheses, sometimes at the expence of coherence and clarity.[7]

Here now is Saint-Gelais's adaptation of the same material from Ariosto:

> Si j'ay du bien, hélas! c'est par mensonge;
> Et mon torment est pure vérité.
> Je n'ay douceur qu'en dormant et en songe
> Et en veillant je n'ay qu'austerité:
> Le jour m'est mal, et bien l'obscurité:
> Le court sommeil Madame me presente,
> Et le resveil la fait trouver absente,
> Ha! povres yeux, où estes vous reduits?
> Clos vous voyez tout ce qui vous contente,
> Et descouverts ne voyez rien qu'ennuis.
>
> (Blanchemain, I, 107)

Saint-Gelais, too, injects into the Italian antitheses the contrast of presence and absence. Here, however, that contrast is firmly related to the distinction between sleep and waking (already well defined by the opening lines), and no confusion arises. Better articulated, the dizain also unfolds in such a way as to render each line syntactically independent. As a result, the antitheses receive further emphasis, and Saint-Gelais demonstrates the ability to excel in the epigrammatic vein that so enchanted his contemporaries.

It may be argued at this point that Du Bellay's dismissal of "Laissez la verde couleur" involves the lyric mode, not epigrammatic verse, and that the comparison between Saint-Gelais and Ronsard which opens this chapter shows Mellin at a singular disadvantage before Ronsard's dramatic lyricism. Also, we have yet to observe Mellin at work in that realm of expression where, to use Pasquier's expression, poets sought "de plus contenter leurs esprits, que l'opinion du commun peuple." Saint-Gelais and Ronsard, Saint-Gelais and Du Bellay do come together in such a context, however, now in adaptations from Claudian and Menander, now in a version of Horace's "Diffugere nives," all sources for revealing contrasts.

The Claudian text that attracted both Saint-Gelais and Ronsard is the famous "De sene Veronensi qui suburbium numquam egressus est." Menander's poem Saint-Gelais studied in the Latin adaptation by Navagero entitled "Ex Maenandro." Saint-Gelais renders each work in a straightforward fashion, whereas Ronsard's reworking of Claudian forms but a small portion of a long piece addressed to the Cardinal de Châtillon. Elements of the Latin work are transposed or omitted, and the adaptation eventually moves away from Claudian's theme of the satisfaction of the old man from Verona with his native home towards the man's preference for his country existence over life at the court. Ronsard's reprise of Menander is called simply "A lui-mesme," meaning, to Magny, to whom the previous poem in the collection is addressed. Again, the thrust of the classical poem (man must recognize his place in the scheme of things) acquires a new context as Ronsard makes a reference to what Magny is seeking from the King and urges his friend to take heart.

Some modern readers will doubtlessly feel that Ronsard's treatment bespeaks the greater creative force, that is, a capacity to mould his borrowings, whereas Saint-Gelais barely rises above the level of a schoolroom exercise in translation. But mid-sixteenth-century views on translation were far from simple. Sébillet raised translation to the status of a veritable poetic genre (Art poétique, II, xiv), incurring Du Bellay's wrath

(*Deffence*, I, vi). In addition, as recent scholars have been quick to point out, theory and practice on translation often did not coincide.[8] Sonnets in *L'Olive* translate more than one Italian source. The case of Ronsard's *Hinne de Bacus*, printed with a Latin translation by Dorat on facing pages, must come to mind again. Even within the world of the Pléiade close translation was practiced and, on occasion, advertised. Saint-Gelais did no less, but "Laissez la verde couleur" proves that Mellin was also perfectly capable of treating borrowed material in the free and creative fashion required by the *Deffence*. Saint-Gelais's adaptation of Second's sixth basium can show us yet another example of the same phenomenon.

Called "Douze baisers gaignés au jeu" (Blanchemain, I, 200-03), Saint-Gelais's poem contains 96 verses in *rimes plates*. Imitation of Second begins only at line 50, with sustained imitation commencing at line 69. Here several pertinent and graceful turns of phrase capture the essence of the Latin. For

> Cùm pius irrorat sitienteis Iuppiter agros,
>   Deciduæ guttas non numeramus aquæ.
> Sic quoque cùm Borea nimbosus inhorruit aër,
>   Sumpsit & irata Iuppiter arma manu,
> Grandine confusa terras, & cærula pulsat,
>   Nescius inuertat quot sata, quotue locis
>
>   (p. 10)

Saint-Gelais writes,

> Quand Jupiter la terre seiche arrose,
> Ou que le ciel à orage il dispose,
> On ne va point compter la gresle toute,
> Ny calculer la pluye goutte à goutte.

The Latin

> Tu quoque cum Dea sis diua formosior illa,
>   Concha per æquoreum quam uaga ducit iter,
> Basia cur numero, cœlestia dona, coarctas
>
>   (p. 10)

becomes

> Vous donc, amie, en beauté comparée
> A l'immortelle et blonde Cytherée,
> Que n'usez-vous de liberalité
> Appartenante à immortalité?
> Pourquoy nous sont les graces départies
> De vos baisers par comptes et parties?

To introduce this material Saint-Gelais imagines a promise between poet and lady assuring him twelve kisses. She has to date granted him only six, the source of a reference to the lady's annoying propensity for counting her favors, and the heart of Second's theme. The ensuing lines contain, for those who have read extensively in the love verse of the day, only too familiar clichés. But again certain passages have an unmistakable sureness:

> Car pensez-vous qu'une bouche vermeille,
> Bien qu'elle rende heureux l'œil et l'oreille
> Par un doux ris et parler gracieux,
> Puisse nourrir un cœur ambitieux
> De ce seul bien . . . .

And Saint-Gelais never forgets his theme:

> Douze est bien peu au prix de l'infini,
> Dont mon desir doit estre diffini.
> Car, quand j'aurois cent mille fois baisé,
> Mon cœur encor' ne seroit appaisé.
> Amour est Dieu, et nous fumée et ombre,
> Ne luy saurions satisfaire par nombre.

If we return now to Saint-Gelais's translations from Claudian and Menander, it will be interesting to see whether his style can compare favorably with the lines that Ronsard wrote upon reading the same Latin verses.

Here are the opening lines of Saint-Gelais's "D'un vieillard d'auprès Véronne, traduict de Claudien":

> O bien-heureux qui a passé son aage
> Dedans le clos de son propre héritage,
> Et n'a de vue eslongné sa maison
> En jeunes ans, et en vieille saison;

> Qui d'un baston et du bras secouru
> Va par les champs où jeune il a couru,
> Les siecles longs pas à pas racontant[9]
> Du tect champestre où il est habitant.
>   Nul accident d'inconstante fortune
> Luy a monstré sa fureur importune,
> Ny a esté par peines et dangers
> Sa soif estaindre aux fleuves estrangers.
>   (Blanchemain, I, 63)

Now Ronsard's version:

> O bien heureux celuy qui peut user son age
> En repos, labourant son petit heritage!
> Qui loing de ses enfants, charitable, ne part,
> Qu'une mesme maison a veu jeune & vieillart,
> Et qui par les moissons au printemps retournées,
> Et non pas par les Roys, va contant les années,
> Qui se soutient les bras d'un baston appuyez
> Parmi les champs où jeune alloit à quatre pieds,
> Qui voit les grans forets, qu'il plantoit en jeunesse,
> D'un mesme age que luy parvenir à vieillesse.
>   (*Oeuvres complètes*, X, 12)

Even with the advantage of the alexandrin, Ronsard must invent the *cheville* "Qui loing de ses enfants, charitable, ne part." His vivid rendering of "in qua reptavit harena" ("Parmi les champs où jeune alloit à quatre pieds") is well matched by the elegance of Saint-Gelais's "Sa soif estaindre aux fleuves estrangers" ("nec bibit ignotas . . . aquas").

The two versions of Navagero's Latin translation from Menander are interesting primarily because Ronsard begins with the same crisp style so characteristic of Saint-Gelais:

> Lors que ta mere estoit preste à gesir de toi,
> Si Jupiter, des Dieus & des hommes le roi,
> Lui eust juré ces mots: l'enfant dont tu es pleine
> Sera tant qu'il vivra sans douleur & sans peine,
> Et tousjours lui viendront les biens sans y songer, —
> Tu dirois à bon droit Jupiter mensonger.
>   (*Oeuvres complètes*, VI, 120)

But, whereas Saint-Gelais maintains the same tone throughout, Ronsard does not. The Latin phrase "si eisdem legibus / Quibus nos omnes (tragicis ut uerbis loquar) / Aeque patentem cunctis aerem trahis," is rendered by Saint-Gelais as "Mais si tu vis en cest air ample et large / Sous mesmes loix que nous, et mesme charge" (Blanchemain, I, 249). Ronsard likewise omits the parentheses, but then embellishes extravagantly on the thought of the phrase:

> Mais puis que tu es né, ainsi que tous nous sommes,
> A la condition des miserables hommes,
> Pour avoir en partage ennuis, soucis, travaus,
> Douleurs, tristesses, soins, tormans, peines & maus
>
> . . . .
> (*Oeuvres complètes*, VI, 120-21)

When we reach the concluding portion of the Latin text, Saint-Gelais succeeds in framing his verses in such a way as to permit the rhymes to accentuate Menander's message. The person addressed must

> Considerer, ami, que tu es homme;
> Qui est de tous l'animal plustost mis
> Au haut degré et le plustost desmis;
> Et à bon droict, car il est de nature
> De peu de force, et foible creature;
> Et toutefois, ainsi debile et tendre.
> (Blanchemain, I, 249)

The parallelism in "plustost mis"/"plustost desmis," the linking of "de nature" and "foible creature" serve each to reinforce essential points. Ronsard is much less successful in this regard. Magny will bear the effects of fortune, he says,

> Quand quelque fois le jour en ton cœur penseras
> Que tu n'es que pur homme, & qu'on ne voit au monde
> Chose qui plus que l'homme en miseres abonde,
> Qui plus soudain s'éleve, & qui plus soudain soit
> Tombé quand il est haut; & certes à bon droit,
> Car il n'a point de force, & si tousjours demande
> D'atenter, plus que lui, quelque entreprise grande.
> (*Oeuvres complètes*, VI, 121)

The contrast between "s'éleve" and "soit / Tombé" seems all the more awkward, given the repetition of "plus soudain." The adverbial phrase leads us to expect that the word balancing "s'éleve" will come at the end of the line, but it does not. Perhaps Ronsard hoped to achieve his effect through the enjambement of "Tombé," a falling, so to speak, from the preceding line. If so, the clause that follows the past participle dilutes the effect. How much more successful, for example, is Du Bellay's technique in these lines from *Les Antiquités*: "Le Tybre seul, qui vers la mer s'enfuit, / Reste de Rome."

Ronsard's reputation will not stand or fall upon the worth of these few lines taken from Claudian and Menander. In a poet whose total production extends over so many pages, some unevenness is inevitable. The revelation I would stress comes on the side of Saint-Gelais, whose range and talent beyond the epigrammatic mode emerge with particular sharpness when we consider how other poets of the day responded to the same foreign models. In this regard few potential contrasts between Saint-Gelais and the Pléiade prove so telling as the one occasioned by Mellin's and Du Bellay's adaptations of the Horatian ode "Diffugere nives."

Here are the texts of Horace and Saint-Gelais:

> Diffugere nives, redeunt iam gramina campis
>   arboribusque comae;
> mutat terra vices et decrescentia ripas
>   flumina praetereunt;
> Gratia cum Nymphis geminisque sororibus audet
>   ducere nuda choros.
> Immortalia ne speres, monet annus et almum
>   quae rapit hora diem:
> frigora mitescunt Zephyris, ver proterit aestas,
>   interitura simul
> pomifer autumnus fruges effuderit, et mox
>   bruma recurrit iners.
> Damna tamen celeres reparant caelestia lunae:
>   nos ubi decidimus
> quo pater Aeneas, quo Tullus dives et Ancus,
>   pulvis et umbra sumus.
> Quis scit an adiciant hodiernae crastina summae

tempora di superi?
Cuncta manus avidas fugient heredis, amico
    quae dederis animo.
Cum semel occideris et de te splendida Minos
    fecerit arbitria,
non, Torquate, genus, non te facundia, non te
    restituet pietas.
Infernis neque enim tenebris Diana pudicum
    liberat Hippolytum,
nec Lethaea valet Theseus abrumpere caro
    vincula Pirithoo.

                    (IV, vii)

Imitation
près de translation d'une ode d'Horace

     Or ha hyver, avecques sa froidure,
     Quicté le lieu à la belle verdure
        Qui painct les arbrisseaux;
     La terre change accoustrements nouveaux,
5   Et ne sont plus si non petits ruisseaux
        Les tant grosses rivières.
     Les vois-tu jà, nues, en ces bruières,
     Chanter, danser les Graces familières,
        Et les nymphes des bois?
10   Ce changement de l'an tel que tu vois,
     Te monstre, amy, si bien tu le cognois,
        Que rien n'est immuable.
     L'hyver s'en va au retour souhaictable
     Du doux Printemps, qui de l'Esté aymable
15   Tantost surprins sera;
     Automne après sur l'Esté se ruera,
     Et puis l'Hyver le siege levera
        Au fructueux Automne.
     Au cours des temps la lune belle et bonne,
20   Sans leur faillir, si certain ordre donne
        Qu'ils en sont remis sus;
     Mais aussitost que sommes rués jus
     Là où Roland et Lancelot sont cheus
        Rien que pouldre ne sommes.
25   Puis en est-il un seul entre tant d'hommes
     Qui soit certain que Dieu croistra les sommes
        De ses jours d'un demain?

Entretien doncq le tien amy humain;
Car tel acquest ne peut tomber en main
30   De tes biens héritière,
Qui pourriront aussi bien que ta biere;
Mais ton bienfaict sera mis en lumiere
Et loing esclairera,
Tant que clarté sera.
(Blanchemain, I, 81-82)

Saint-Gelais remains very close to his source, yet not so close that we find no reworking of the original. The names of Roland and Lancelot are substituted for Aeneas, Tullus and Ancus; the ending abandons Horace's final four lines altogether, and lines 32-34 recast a negative statement by the Latin poet regarding Torquatus' inability to resuscitate himself after death and produce a positive observation on the capacity of kindness to continue to shine long after our earthly goods have perished.

Although the notion of poetry outlasting the ravages of time is hardly original among sixteenth-century poets, it is interesting that Du Bellay decided to end "Du retour du printens" with this theme:

Ce grand tour violant
De l'an leger-volant
Ravist & jours & moys:
Non les doctes escriz,
Qui sont de noz espris
Les perdurables voix.
(*Oeuvres*, III, 36)

Could it just be that Du Bellay studied "Or ha hyver" before writing his own ode, preferring as he does to replace Horace's ending with a statement that imitates Saint-Gelais in its emphasis on a facet of human action that outlives mortal man?[10] Whether Du Bellay did or did not consult "Or ha hyver," his version of the Latin ode proves flattering to Saint-Gelais. If the parallel was conscious, then Du Bellay had acknowledged the validity of Saint-Gelais's insight; if it was not, we observe in yet another context a closeness in procedure between two literary worlds the *Deffence* attempts to keep rather separate.

Of equal interest is the fact that Du Bellay not only uses his poem to praise an acquaintance (Dorat), but, like Saint-Gelais, also suppresses the numerous classical references in Horace. "Du retour du printens" contains passages borrowed from more than one Horatian ode, but vv. 45-54 echo with precision that portion of the *carmen* which includes reference to Aeneas, Tullus and Ancus and which could have led to Horace's evocation of Diana, Hippolytus and Pirithous. All are abandoned in favor of a simple restatement of Horace's broad observations:

> Mais les lunes volaiges
> Ces celestes dommaiges
> Reparent: & nous hommes,
> Quand descendons aux lieux
> De noz ancestres vieux,
> Umbre & poudre nous sommes.
> Pourquoy doncq' avons-nous envie
> Du soing qui les cœurs ronge & fend?
> Le terme bref de notre vie
> Long espoir nous deffent.
>   (*Oeuvres*, III, 35-36)

As with "Laissez la verde couleur," we see again that the presence of erudition cannot always be used to distinguish between a Saint-Gelais composition and that of a Pléiade poet.

At the same time, the two adaptations of "Diffugere nives" do differ with respect to the form employed. For his three-line stanzas, Saint-Gelais chose a rhyme scheme that binds each stanza to its predecessor: aab, bbc, ccd, and so forth, a procedure that does not point to the lyric stanza to come. "Du retour du printens," on the other hand, conforms in every respect to the new emerging lyric structure. Its dizains are constructed of five rhymes whose alternation remains constant without any rhyme being repeated in the succeeding stanza. Were we ever inclined to use such a difference to establish a firm distinction between the Pléiade and its "less talented" contemporaries, the preceding discussion should suffice to restrain us, and, in point of fact, when we examine the way in which each poet responds to the Latin original, we find that Saint-Gelais's text gives continued proof of his ability to practice the lyric as well as the epigrammatic mode.

Consider, for example, the poets' respective versions of the seasonal cycle and its lesson:

Saint-Gelais	Du Bellay
L'hyver s'en va au retour souhaictable	Voici, deja l'eté qui tonne
Du doux Printemps, qui de l'Esté [aymable	Chasse le peu durable ver,
Tantost surprins sera;	
Automne après sur l'Esté se ruera,	L'eté le fructueux autonne,
Et puis l'Hyver le siege levera	L'autonne le frilleux hyver.
Au fructueux Automne.	
Au cours des temps la lune belle et [bonne,	Mais les lunes volaiges
Sans leur faillir, si certain ordre donne	Ces celestes dommaiges
Qu'ils en sont remis sus;	Reparent: & nous hommes,
Mais aussitost que sommes rués jus	Quand descendons aux lieux
Là où Roland et Lancelot sont cheus	De noz ancestres vieux,
Rien que pouldre ne sommes.	Umbre & poudre nous sommes.

More than once Du Bellay imitates Horace so closely as to produce a text that is best understood only through reference to the original Latin. Would "lunes volaiges" (for "celeres . . . lunae") and "celestes dommaiges" (for "Damna . . . caelestia") be otherwise clear, even after several readings? (And, regarding clarity, it must be pointed out that reason, not Du Bellay's word order, tells us that "le fructueux autonne" and "le frilleux hyver" are the subjects of their respective elliptical clauses, not the direct objects, as they might appear at first glance.)

Saint-Gelais's version poses no such problems, even though Mellin reworks Horace's imagery in key verses. The phrases and verbs used in his poem to describe the succession of the seasons ("surprins sera," "se ruera," "le siege levera"), for example, seem to have been carefully chosen to prepare the image used to render "Damna tamen celeres reparant caelestia lunae": "ils en sont remis sus" (restored to strength).

Mere details? If so, they are details that reveal an appealing desire to imitate and at the same time to recast and recreate. Can Du Bellay's single verb, "Chasse," and string of adjectives, "peu durable," "fructueux," "frilleux" be said to capture the poetic energy of Horace's "proterit . . . interitura . . . recurrit"? At the same time, it should be noted that Horace's verbs establish no single pattern. Only "proterit" suggests one season's forceful supplanting of another. Not only does Saint-Gelais preserve the vividness of the Latin poem at this point, but he also insists upon creating a metaphorical coherence that is quite appropriate to the meaning of Horace's ode, yet entirely independent of its specific vocabulary.

How telling, nonetheless, that one of the most recent critical studies to mention Saint-Gelais (an article on George Buchanan)[11] uses a Latin work by Mellin to accentuate the distance between the style of the early sixteenth century, described as "competent, witty, but unexceptional" (p. 144), and Buchanan's rich, complex diction, frequently Horatian in tone. The possibility for a rehabilitation of Mellin de Saint-Gelais sweeping enough to catapult him into the ranks of the great French poets of the sixteenth century does not exist. The proportion of witty, but frivolous verse he penned quite overshadows those few poems in which, as we have seen, other qualities shine forth. In a word, proportions are telling. Yet they do not tell everything. The majesty of the closing stanzas of "Laissez la verde couleur" owes nothing to previous experiments with the Adonis theme, and, similarly, we do not find in Horace so fine a progression in imagery from the successive victories of one season over another to the restoration of each to a position of lost strength. In addition, it should be stressed that, just as Saint-Gelais's success in "Laissez la verde couleur" includes surmounting the demands of a very particular rhyme scheme, the poet achieves comparable success in "Or ha hyver," in which every third verse determines the rhyme of the next two verses. Despite the complex prosody, the reader feels no constraint or excess in either case. Henry Guy's phrase regarding the Rhétoriqueurs ("c'est justement parce qu'ils n'ont rien à dire, qu'ils parlent avec tant de recherche," I, 381) seems inappropriate to describe either poem. Saint-Gelais has something to say in each instance, enough to demonstrate through both the models in question and the independence displayed that, quite as Pasquier suggests, the 1540s are a rich and consequential moment in French literary history. The lyric mode in particular makes important strides, a development of which Saint-Gelais is very much aware. As Becker reminds us, of Saint-Gelais's strophic pieces only "Laissez la verde couleur" appears in Chantilly MS 523. Does this fact not imply that the others were written later, that is, in the 1540s?[12] The best of Saint-Gelais's writing signals other advances that should be noted as well.

One of his adaptations of the Second basia hints, for example, at a recognition of distinct differences between epigrammatic and lyric diction. That he preferred to expend most of his energies on the former, not the latter, separates him, of course, from the Pléiade; however, it is worth observing that virtually all his works selected for analysis in this study were printed in the Oeuvres of 1547[13] and, therefore, composed well in advance of the Deffence. His preoccupation with the epigram notwithstanding, hard evidence exists for the presence in Saint-Gelais of a much wider poetic sense, one that definitely points ahead towards a poetry concerned with criteria other than "l'opinion du commun peuple." It has been to emphasize this fact as forcefully as possible that I have juxtaposed certain pieces by Mellin de Saint-Gelais and the Pléiade, for in his way Saint-Gelais, too, earned the right to appear on the list of forerunners of the new poetry to come.

APPENDIX TO CHAPTER IV

Second, Basium "Centum basia centies"

Centum basia centies,
Centum basia millies,
Mille & basia centies,
Et tot millia millies,
Quot guttæ Siculo mari,
    Quot sunt sidera cœlo,
Istis purpureis genis,
Istis turgidulis labris,
Ocellisǻue loquaculis,
Darem continuo impetu
    Ò formosa Neæra
Sed dum totus inhæreo
Conchatim roseis genis,
Conchatim rutilis labris,
Ocellisǻue loquaculis;
Non datur tua cernere
Labra, non roseas genas,
Ocellosǻue loquaculos,
    Molleis nec mihi risus:
Qui, uelut nigra discutit
Cœlo, nubila Cynthius,
Pacatumǻue per æthera
Gemmatis in equis micat
    Flauo lucidus orbe:
Sic nutu eminus aureo,
Et meis lachrymas genis,
Et curas animo meo,
    Et suspiria pellunt.
Heu quàm sunt oculis meis
Nata prælia cum labris.
Ergo ego mihi uel Iouem

Riualem potero pati?
Riuales oculi mei
Non ferunt mea labra.
(pp. 12-14)

Chapter V

EPILOGUE:
EDITING SAINT-GELAIS

It is no accident that the most scholarly study of Saint-Gelais yet published includes a detailed discussion of the process whereby his poems gradually reached the public in printed form, as well as a summary of several manuscripts in which poems by Saint-Gelais appear. In his monograph, P.A. Becker wished to communicate, along with such valuable information about our sources for Saint-Gelais's poetry, a sense of the difficulty that surrounds any attempt to identify in these sources the poems that can be attributed beyond any doubt to the poet, a point on which it is possible to expand at some length.

Of the various editions of Saint-Gelais's poetry, only one appeared during his lifetime. Yet the role of the poet (versus the printer) in the preparation of the 1547 collection remains unclear. Becker believes the selection of poems to be "zu willkürlich und zu lückenhaft" (p. 48) to suggest that Saint-Gelais himself provided the poetry presented. Noteworthy also is the absence from the volume of such poems as "De Sainct Gelais sur son livre" and "De lui mesme," which open the collective editions of 1574 and 1719. On the other hand, present as the concluding section of the 1547 volume is a series of poems introduced by "Laissez la verde couleur" and this revealing rubric: "Chanson Elegie, ou Chanson lamentable de Venus sur la mort de bel Adonis. Par S.G. Avec plusieurs compositions, tant de B. des Periers, que d'autres poetes François" (p. 49). Despite the book's title (*Saingelais, Oeuvres de luy . . .*), only part of the 1547 volume contains poems by Mellin; elsewhere we are once again dealing with a collection of verse by largely unidentified authors in the vein of the *Hecatomphile*, in which Saint-Gelais's "Description d'Amour" appeared for the first time, or Du Moulin's *Déploration* of 1545, which marks the first appearance in print of "Laissez la verde couleur." The relationship between the first collected edition of Saint-Gelais's poetry and Du Moulin's volume goes even deeper. Of the 21 poems printed in 1547 after "Laissez la verde couleur," no fewer than seventeen are already present in the Du Moulin *Déploration* of 1545 and, with one exception, printed in the same order.[1] That Du Moulin's publication of 1545 with "Laissez la verde couleur" at its beginning may have stimulated another printer to profit from his work,[2] yet disguise the effort with added works by Saint-Gelais, seems an inescapable possibility, a possibility which has important overtones with respect to the accuracy of the text reproduced and the general presentation of the material.

The 1547 edition makes no attempt at a strict grouping of the poems. The longer works tend to precede the shorter poems (but there are exceptions), and translations appear at irregular intervals among the original works. The 1574 *Oeuvres poétiques de Mellin de S. Gelais* offers a very different format. After the two short poems by Saint-Gelais on his work just mentioned, a general category "Opuscules" begins, containing poetry for various court fêtes. (Since these events postdate 1547, the absence of such poems from the first edition can be readily explained.) Then the longer poems on diverse subjects, including Saint-Gelais's translations, appear, much in the haphazard plan of 1547. The shorter pieces (sonnets, rondeaux, ballades, quatrains, sizains, and so forth) follow, with the épitaphes, élégies, two translations entitled épigrammes, épistres, énigmes and chansons reproduced at the very end. This grouping deserves some attention since it is in the main the same grouping observed by MSS B.N. fr. 878 and 885, about which Becker has written that they can "nur auf den Dichter selbst zurückgehen, weil er allein in dieser Weise über das vollständige Material gebot" (p. 47). This grouping is maintained in the 1719 edition through p. 225, at which point are added "Vers de Mellin de S. Gelais non imprimez jusqu'à présent." Here his French poems appear first, in no particular order, followed by the Latin verses.

If the 1547 *Oeuvres* seems more likely the inspiration of its printer than of our poet, so the way in which it presents Saint-Gelais's poems intimates that the volume falls outside an alternate and fairly standard grouping of his poems for which the poet may have been responsible. Does this mean that the versions of Saint-Gelais's poetry contained in the *Oeuvres* of 1547 are also suspect? We cannot resolve this problem any more than we can brand Du Moulin's text of the "Déploration" and of "O combien est heureuse" as faulty and inauthentic. We shall see below that the edition of 1547 frequently stands apart from other readings, quite as its special grouping of the poems would suggest, but, since the divergence never becomes absolute or fanciful (as in the case of the poetry printed with song books), we cannot dismiss the volume when studying the body of Saint-Gelais's poetry. As a result, the edition admirably illustrates important collateral aspects of the general problem that Becker wished to raise.

Although within both the manuscript and printed text traditions a definite format can be found for presenting Saint-Gelais's poems, the one modern edition of those works obscures this fact. Blanchemain printed first the texts of 1547, which, of course, do not contain the numerous pièces de circonstance that predominate at the opening of the traditional sequence. When Blanchemain then reproduced the texts of the 1574 edition, he omitted those poems already reprinted from the earliest edition and further masked the traditional sequence. Were one to contemplate reediting Saint-Gelais, identifying this sequence proves to be the only easy aspect of the task, however. The questions of which poems to include and which version of certain poems to offer present very vexing problems indeed.

One of these questions has already been addressed. When reviewing Becker's monograph, which doubts that Saint-Gelais composed all the works reprinted by Blanchemain, Plattard extended the number of poems of questionable authorship appearing in the Blanchemain edition to include 53 more pieces. A 1924 article by Pierre Jourda adds further texts to the list. Yet even were it possible to establish with certainty the corpus of Saint-Gelais's poetry, there remains the question of which version of many of these poems to reproduce.

Let us consider, for example, the case of "Laissez la verde couleur" and "O combien est heureuse." Although both appear in Blanchemain's edition as part of the 1547 printing of Saint-Gelais's poetry, the text furnished by Blanchemain for "Laissez la verde couleur" is actually that of the 1574 edition. The text of "O combien est heureuse" comes from the 1719 edition of the poet's *Oeuvres*. ("O combien est heureuse" was not included in the 1574 edition.) Since neither of these editions could have been prepared under Saint-Gelais's direction, the reasons for Blanchemain's choice must remain obscure, all the more so since the version of each poem appearing in the 1574 or 1719 edition corresponds to no clear pattern among the variants I have collated.

Even if we set aside obvious typographical errors in the many printings of the poems, we still find a singular variety in the way the two poems were offered. Some variants point to a strong uniformity among the texts printed after 1545 ("Laissez la verde couleur": vv. 32, 39, 40, 42, 43, 71, 108, 138; "O combien est heureuse": vv. 22, 49); others point to the very opposite, that is, to passages of distinct uncertainty ("Laissez la verde couleur": vv. 22, 28, 51, 62, 63, 65, 76, 110, 135; "O combien est heureuse": vv. 12, 32, 36, 38, 44, 52—not to mention variation in the number and arrangement of the stanzas). Some variants show interesting pairings among the various texts collated. The variants in vv. 12, 28, 33, 74, 75, 76, 79, 124 and 156 of "Laissez la verde couleur" point to striking parallels between MSS B.N. n. a. fr. 1158 and Chantilly 523. Variants in vv. 110, 142, 144 and 148 of the same poem suggest an affiliation among the c. 1550 *Recueil des chansons, tant musicales que rurales*, the 1555 *Recueil de toutes les sortes de chansons nouvelles* and the Du Moulin reprint of 1561. This affiliation emphasizes anew the ever-present link between republication of "Laissez la verde couleur" and the vogue of the chanson, but it also helps to explain why the Du Moulin volume of 1561 departs from the generally careful presentation of the poem in the other Du Moulin editions. In the case of "O combien est heureuse," variants for vv. 6, 7, 9, 32, 36, 43 and 52 imply a relationship between the Du Moulin reprinting of 1556 and MS B.N. fr. 885, to which the Sébillet text of 1548 also bears some resemblance (cf. variants for vv. 9, 11, 32, 43). Better informed by these facts about the complexity of poets' and printers' ways in the early sixteenth century, we remain, nevertheless, no nearer to the answer to the question: which text reproduces Saint-Gelais's final touches?

A number of other poems illustrate the same difficulty, even though the works in question achieved a far smaller success than the opening selections of Du Moulin's *Déploration*.

In Blanchemain's edition, "Ces six œillets" appears among the poems reprinted from the 1547 volume of Saint-Gelais's works. The poem is a douzain and runs as follows:

> Ces six œillets, mesliez en ceste guise,
> Vous sont par moy ce matin envoyés,
> Pour vous monstrer, par ceux de couleur grise,
> Que j'ay du mal plus que vous n'en voyez;
> Vous suppliant que vous y pourvoyez.
> Les rouges sont plaincte, en l'autre moitié,
> Non point de vous, mais du Dieu sans pitié,
> Qui de mon sang prend vie et nourriture;
> Et tous ensemble, ayans de leur nature
> Breve saison, vous portent ce message
> Que la beauté est un bien qui peu dure,
> Et que qui l'ha la doit mettre en usage.
>   (Blanchemain, I, 110)

Although Blanchemain's preliminary material states, "La présente édition commence par une réimpression du texte de ce précieux volume [de 1547]" (I, 33), in truth the 1547 version of "Ces six œillets" is a huitain (which explains why the title above the Blanchemain text reads "Autre"; the poem repeats the form of its predecessor, a huitain):

> Ces six oeilletz meslez en ceste guise
> Vous sont par moy ce matin enuoyez
> Pour vous monstrer à la liurée grise
> Que i'ay du mal plus que vous ne croyez,
> Et que de brief si vous n'y pouruoyez
> On me verra pis encore endurer,
> C'est le subiect des fleurs que vous voyez
> Dont la verdeur ne peut guere durer.
>   (pp. 39-40)

In MSS B.N. fr. 878 (f. 113r-v) and 885 (f. 117v), the poem appears as a douzain, quite as Blanchemain prints it, with the exception of the variants "meslez" in line 1 and "font" in line 6. These variant spellings are retained in the editions of 1574 and 1719, in which the poem is also a douzain. Clearly, the poem exists in two versions, and both texts should be included in any critical edition of Saint-Gelais's poetry.

Mellin's adaptation of the seventh basium of Second, a work already discussed above, appears in the Blanchemain edition in the following form:

> Cent mille fois et en cent mille sortes
> Je baiserois ceste bouche et ces yeux,
> Lors que mes mains plus que les vostres fortes,
> Vous rendent prise, et moy victorieux;
> Mais, en baisant, mon œil trop curieux
> De voir le bien que ma bouche luy cache,
> Se tire arriere et seul à jouïr tâche,
> De la beauté qu'il perd quand elle y touche:
> Devinez donc si autre ami me fâche,
> Puis que mes yeux sont jaloux de ma bouche.
>   (Blanchemain, I, 104)

Though included with other poems from the 1547 edition, the wording Blanchemain chose again conforms in reality to the text published in the *Oeuvres* of 1574 and 1719 (in essence, the version found in MS B.N. fr. 878, f. 98v). When analyzing the work, I reproduced the text as it appears in a Paris 1550 volume entitled *Traductions de latin en francoys, imitations, et inventions nouvelles, tant de Clement Marot, que d'autres des plus excellens poëtes de ce temps* (sig. F6r). This version differs from Blanchemain's text in three respects:

> De la beauté qu'il perd quand *il* y touche
> Deuinez doncq' *s'vn* autre amy me fasche
> Puys que *mon oeil est* ialoux de ma bouche.

The third variant does not alter the sense of the work; it does, however, effect a greater uniformity of expression within the epigram, since, although reference is made to the lady's "yeux," the poet refers previously, when speaking of himself, to "[s]on œil." The variant "il" for "elle" in vs. 8 does change the meaning of the line. As printed by Blanchemain, the work alludes to the beauty lost by the eye when "elle," the poet's mouth, kisses the beloved. The text of 1550 refers to the beauty lost by the eye when *it* draws near the lady. This version is much less satisfying in view of the general theme of the rivalry between eye and mouth ("mon œil trop curieux / De voir le bien que ma bouche luy cache"). Still, it is interesting to observe that our sources offer little uniformity regarding this line,[3] quite in the manner of certain passages from "Laissez la verde couleur."

The sonnet "Voyant ces monts de veue ainsi loingtaine," whose place in literary history has to date derived from the fact that it shows Saint-Gelais imitating the English poet Thomas Wyatt,[4] exists in at least three versions. The poem is printed by Blanchemain as part of the 1547 edition of the *Oeuvres*. Yet again we are misled. Here is the text of the 1547 edition:

> Voyant ces monts de veue ainsi loingtaine
> Ie les compare à mon long desplaisir,
> Hault est leur chief, & hault est mon desir,
> Leur pié est ferme & m'amour est certaine:
> Là mainct ruisseau court & mainte fontaine,
> De mes deux yeulx sortent pleurs à plaisir,
> De grands souspirs ne me puis dessaisir
> Et de grands vents leur sime est toute pleine:
> Mille trouppeaux y prennent leur pasture,
> Amour en moy prend vie & nourriture:
> En eulx sans fruict fueilles ont apparence,
> I'ay sans effect assez bonne esperance,
> Et d'eulx à moy n'ha qu'vne diference
> Qu'en eulx la neige, en moy la flamme dure.
>
> (p. 19)

Blanchemain offers us the work essentially as it appears in MS B.N. fr. 878 (f. 91r-v), where after small variants in the quatrains

1547	*MS B.N. fr. 878*
m'amour est certaine	ma foy est certaine

Là . . . court	D'eulx . . . coule
à plaisir	a loisir
De grands	De fortz

significant differences emerge in the tercets:

. . . s'y promenent et paissent
Autant d'Amours se couuent et renaissent
Dedans mon coeur qui seul est ma[5] Pasture
Ilz sont sans fruict[;] mon bien n'est qu'apparence.

Finally, in Chantilly MS 523 (f. 221[r]), we find a text that agrees now with MS B.N. fr. 878 (vv. 4, 5 ["coule" only], 6), now with the edition of 1547 (vv. 5 [Là], 7, tercets), yet it adds an alternate reading of its own in vs. 1: "prochaine" for "loingtaine."

Since we know Saint-Gelais's source and have sufficient means to state that the works in which the three versions are found come in the chronological order (1) MS 523, (2) *Oeuvres*, 1547, (3) MS B.N. fr. 878,[6] if we hypothesize for a moment that the three versions represent successive redactions, we discover that the supposition cannot be sustained with equal force throughout the poem. Although the "earliest" reading, "Voyant ces monts de veue ainsi prochaine," could be said to have given way to the "definitive" form, "de veue ainsi loingtaine," in order to bring the poem into closer harmony with the English model ("vnmeasurable montayns"), the "definitive" readings for vs. 4 ("ma foy est certaine") and vs. 5 ("coule") appear already in the Chantilly manuscript. Here the *Oeuvres* of 1547 proves to be only an exception, an alternative.

Our hypothesis would require also that the tercets of the Chantilly manuscript and of the *Oeuvres* of 1547 gave way over time to the "definitive" redaction contained in MS B.N. fr. 878. If that is so, Saint-Gelais had a curious change of heart.

The corresponding lines in Wyatt run:

Small fruyt and many leves their toppes do atyre;

. . . .

Cattell in theim; and in me love is fed.

Can it be disputed that the version "En eulx sans fruict fueilles ont apparence" conveys more completely both the English text and the desired antithesis than does "Ilz sont sans fruict[;] mon bien n'est qu'apparence"? In this latter version, we must equate hills ("Ilz") with the promise of fruit—not an obvious assumption—whereas the former version, like Wyatt's poem, builds upon the more logical expectation of fruit from trees flowering on the hillsides.

The 1547 version renders the cattle image in Saint-Gelais's clear epigrammatic style: "Mille trouppeaux y prennent leur pasture, / Amour en moy prend vie & nourriture." MS B.N. fr. 878 becomes rather precious. Love is replaced by a number of Cupids equal to the quantity of grazing flocks; the symmetry of "trouppeaux/y/pasture // Amour/en moy/vie & nourriture," so faithful to the thrust of the English model, disappears entirely as the contrast is spread over three verses instead of two. Of course, our preference for one version over another need not in any way correspond to Saint-Gelais's own feelings. Was it perhaps essential to rework the tercets in order to achieve the more regular CCD EED rhyme scheme? Unfortunately, we have no means to know what his feelings were, and these remarks on the tercets of "Voyant ces monts" accentuate again some of the perplexing issues lurking in the all too numerous variants provided by Saint-Gelais's poetry.

These examples could be multiplied many times.[7] To be sure, some readings fall into the category of scribal slips and typographical errors. Moreover, regarding the poems printed in collections of musical chansons, we know that composers were notorious for the liberties taken when setting poetry to music. But even if we leave these phenomena aside, important difficulties remain. An edition of the major poems such as the translations from Claudian, Horace and Menander, the "Epitaphe d'une belette," "Douze baisers gaignés au jeu," among others, would be feasible, but in the realm of the shorter works considerable frustration awaits the soul that would take up such a task.

NOTES

Chapter I

1. Such abbreviated references are used throughout for titles appearing in the Select Bibliography, pp. 121-23.

2. Du Bellay's list of "episseries" includes the chanson as well as the ballade, rondeau, chant royal and virelai. Our discussion will show that, unlike these four forms, the chanson undergoes in the early decades of the sixteenth century such sustained development that it ceases to be associated with any particular poetic configuration. Moreover, to what exactly Du Bellay is referring in Book II, chapter iv, when he uses the term "chansons vulgaires," proves very difficult to define. (See pp. 27-39). As a result, when speaking here of the "medieval *formes fixes*," I do not include the chanson.

3. Interesting corroboration of this fact is provided by the career of both Marot and Charles Fontaine. The vast majority of Marot's rondeaux and ballades were published in 1532. Thereafter his interest in these genres waned perceptibly. Thanks to a study by Grace Frank of a Vatican manuscript of Fontaine's poetry, we know that his rondeaux, ballades and chants royaux, too, date from the 1530s. See "The Early Work of Charles Fontaine," *Modern Philology*, 23 (1925-1926), 47-60. Equally pertinent here is a poem by François Habert printed in 1545 and entitled *Déploration poétique de feu M. Antoine du Prat*. A segment of the poem concerns the poet's potential invoking of the Muses to sing Prat's praises. Each will use a different genre. The segment includes none of the "episseries":

> Et en grauant ses louanges diffuses,
> Inuoqueray à mon secours les Muses.
> L'vne en fera epigramme en dix vers,
> Disant qu'à tort il est mangé de vers.
>
> .   .   .   .
>
> L'autre dira en fluente elegie,
> De bonnes moeurs sa nature regie,
> L'autre en fera vn grand œuure heroique,
> L'autre escrira en façon Bucolique,
> Et chantera, que Berger de son temps
> Rendra n'ha peu les hommes plus contens.
>
> (p. 15)

4. Of some interest in this regard is the difference in reaction to Pasquier's list between Arthur Tilley and Paul Laumonier. Tilley believes that the ensuing discussion is illustrative: "Beza is here by virtue of his play, *Abraham sacrifiant* (1550), which became very popular" ("From Marot," p. 145). Laumonier seems to feel, as I do, that the discussion may not be illustrative. He associates Pasquier's inclusion of Bèze in the list with a work that pre-dates the Pléiade, to wit, the *Poemata*, but then dismisses Pasquier's judgment in view of the mediocre quality of the verse in that collection:

"s'il fallait compter Bèze parmi les précurseurs de la Pléiade, d'autres poètes latins de France mériteraient également ce titre ..." (*Commentaire*, p. 147). For mv own position on this matter, see p. 68.

5. See Richmond L. Hawkins, *Maistre Charles Fontaine parisien* (Cambridge, Mass., 1916), p. 233, and Caroline Ruutz-Rees, *Charles de Sainte-Marthe (1512-1555)* (New York, 1910), pp. 222-26.

Chapter II

1. See p. 54.

2. See the reprint of Denisot, *Noelz par le conte d'Alsinoys* (Le Mans, 1847), p. 13. The *Recueil des chansons, tant musicales que rurales* (Paris, 1550?) follows suit with a "Chanson nouvelle Damours, sur le chant ô combien est heureuse la pene de celuy [sic]" (f. 38ʳ). This garbled version of the first lines of Mellin's poem shows the strong affiliation among contemporary song books, since the same mistake appears in a similar collection dated 1548. See p. 54.

3. See Hutton, *The Greek Anthology in France*, pp. 318-20; Molinier, pp. 466-70; and Blanchemain's edition of Saint-Gelais.

4. See pp. 81-82.

5. The text of these translations is printed at the end of this chapter, pp. 55-57.

6. For a detailed discussion of the Italian influence on "Laissez la verde couleur," see pp. 70-71.

7. Reproduced on pp. 57-58.

8. V.-L. Saulnier, "Remarques," p. 16. For the second study, see the Select Bibliography under Saulnier, "Mellin de Saint-Gelais, Pernette du Guillet et l'air 'Conde Claros.'"

9. Consider such parallels in phrasing between the two texts as the following:

1530	Cantilena
uidit interemptum	interemptum uidit
Nuperáque purpurantes	nuper purpurantes
Cupidines uocauit	uocauit . . . Cupidines
Adducerent præhensum	Adducerent . . . prehensum
Mox lustra peruolarunt	Mox peruolarunt lustra

10. Why did the poet make so egregious an error in his title for the "Cantilena"? My guess would be that he read either the expanded edition of the *Discours du voyage de Constantinople* or *Le Livre de plusieurs pièces*, in which "Laissez la verde couleur" was followed immediately by "Amour avecques Psyches," printed without the name of the author and with the title "Suite à ladicte fable, prise de l'Espaignol." Knowing Saint-Gelais to have written "Laissez la verde couleur," the poet assumed that Saint-Gelais had also composed its "Suite," a work closely linked to the Greek verses on Adonis by Pseudo-Theocritus. If this assumption is correct, we have a further reason to posit the popularity that Saint-Gelais achieved with "Laissez la verde couleur." At the same time, one cannot help being surprised by the evident desire on the part of the Latin title to relate the "Cantilena" to Saint-Gelais, when the distance between Pseudo-Theocritus' poem and Pernette's adaptation is considerable. Her opening quatrains bear no connection to the Greek model. She reworks the ending and interpolates a punishment for the boar not present in the Greek. The "Cantilena" follows Pseudo-Theocritus, not Pernette, yet insists upon calling attention to a French poet, not its Greek source. The facts thus hint all the

more at some bond between the French poet and those who were writing verse in Latin, a point on which I shall have more to say in the next chapter.

11. *Oeuvres*, ed. C.A. Mayer, vol. V, épigramme CII.

12.   Vos blanches dents ou plustost diamans,
                       Sont la prison des esprits des amans;
                       Et le coral où elles sont encloses,
                       Pallit le teint des plus vermeilles rozes.
                                        (Blanchemain, I, 197)

13. See the strambotti "Della figura de Leontia" and "Della forma de Leontia" and the "Frottole in laude de Leontia" in Baldassarre Olympo da Sassoferrato, *Libro d'amore chiamato Ardelia,* [Venice, 1523], sig. C8ʳ and G6ʳ.

14. Compare these quatrains of a sonnet from the *Opere volgari di Seraphino Aquilano*, Fano [1516]:

                       Se dentro porto una fornace ardente,
                       Et spargo ognhor da gli occhi un largo fiume.
                       hor come il foco & lacqua è si possente,
                       che l'un per laltro mai non si consume?
                       ma sol al mondo amor questo consente
                       che po leuar ciascun di suo costume.
                       & fa che 'l foco suo de l'acqua piglia
                       per farmi exemplo d'ogni merauiglia.
                                        (sig. L6ʳ)

15. A very early identification of the coming of new lyric forms with the French chanson can be found in R. Morçay, "L'Avènement du lyrisme au temps de la Renaissance," *Humanisme et Renaissance*, 3 (1936), 271-88. In his "Aspects littéraires," Georges Dottin goes so far as to propose that in the decade before the *Deffence* a "renouvellement" occurs with regard to poetic themes and style and that, through the setting to music of these new poems, the chanson familiarized the French court with the "renouvellement" in question.

16. Jeffery does not maintain that all the poems he has collected were set to music; however, his critical apparatus fully justifies his claim that for these poems "their connexions with music are stronger" than in the case of the poems contained in the *Jardin de Plaisance* and *La Fleur de Toutes Joyeusetez* (I, 13).

17. Of some interest is the fact that the rhyme scheme of these septains is identical to that used by Michault Taillevent in several of his works, including "Le Passe-Temps," a poem referred to by Fabri in his discussion of the septain. Michault Taillevent does not, however, make of his seventh line a refrain. (On this poet, see Robert Deschaux, *Un Poète bourguignon du XVᵉ siècle: Michault Taillevent, édition et étude* [Geneva, 1975]).

18. The basic rhyme pattern is ababbcc. It is common to all stanzas, save the second, which runs abaccdd.

19. As Dottin further points out (p. lx), the intrusion of a popular style follows rather inevitably from the technique, practiced by Marguerite in the chansons spirituelles, of the *contrafactum*, according to which a profane song was reworked to accommodate a sacred subject (or the reverse). Not only does the presence of this technique in a *recueil* of 1547 accentuate the continued importance of the musical chanson for serious poetry, but, since the majority of the airs Marguerite reworked come from the end of the fifteenth century, it also gives us an insight into one of the ways in which the musical chanson retained its popularity over the years preceding publication of the *Deffence*.

20. See, for example, Lesure, *Musicians*, p. 36. Also, only a cursory glance at Jeffery's two volumes would produce numerous examples of this facet of the early chanson.

21. See vol. III, 173-207, of C.A. Mayer's edition of the *Oeuvres* of Marot. Of some interest are the proportions of strophic chansons (37) to the non-strophic poems (5) and of the strophic chansons that do not repeat the same rhymes throughout (21) to those that do repeat them (16).

22. In "O oppressé suis" (sig. b7^v), stanzas two and three are rhymed ababccaa, but the first stanza has the scheme ababccbb.

23. P.A. Becker's 1924 study of Saint-Gelais contains this observation on the -ée rhyme: "Der durchgehende *ée*-Reim in allen geraden Versen erinnert seltsam an die spanische Romanze und das gewählte Versmass, der Siebensilber, bestärkt den Eindruck" (p. 76). The ballad of *Conde Claros de Montalvan* is composed of heterometric quatrains (three octosyllabic lines followed by one seven-syllable line) in which lines 2 and 4 usually, but not always, contain the same rhyme (-ar). Becker apparently means that the position of the -ée rhyme in Saint-Gelais recalls the -ar rhyme in the ballad. Why he associates the seven-syllable line with the ballad is less clear, since in such poems the octosyllabic line predominates.

24. In "Mellin de Saint-Gelais, Pernette du Guillet et l'air 'Conde Claros,'" p. 531.

25. See the variants printed on pp. 46-49.

26. In his edition of Peletier's *Oeuvres poétiques*, Marcel Françon points out (pp. 348-49) that, when Peletier reworked his seasonal hymns for their 1555 reprinting under the title *L'Amour des amours, vers lyriques*, the reworking results in each ode having stanzas of uniform construction and alternation of masculine and feminine rhymes.

Chapter III

1. Guillaume Des Autels, *Réplique de Guillaume Des Autelz auz furieuses défenses de Louis Maigret* (Lyon, 1551), p. 62.

2. The practice of writing "Merlin" instead of "Mellin" to refer to Saint-Gelais was rather widespread. Peletier uses it again in his "A monsieur de saint-Gelais" (*Oeuvres*, 1547, f. 101^r); Marot does likewise in his "Eglogue de Marot au roy sous les noms de Pan et Robin," vv. 153, 158. A poem by Nicolas Bourbon in the 1538 edition of the *Nugae* is addressed to "Merlinum Sangelasium" (p. 448).

3. On the various ideas that Peletier expressed in advance of the Pléiade, see Laumonier, *Commentaire*, pp. 152-54. When translating Homer, Peletier stressed in particular the necessity to preserve the "maiesté" and "naif" of the original and to convey the force of its adjectives (*Premier et Second Livre de l'Odissee d'Homere* [Paris, 1571], f. 4^v).

4. The poem in question, Du Bellay's adaptation of Dorat's ode on the death of Marguerite de Navarre, inspired further French translations by Ronsard and Baïf.

5. The presence of this particular link between Marot and Salmon Macrin helps us to identify which of the many editions of Marot's psalms inspired the neo-Latin poet. He could not have used a text published after 1542, since in the *Cinquante pseaumes en françois par Clem. Marot* (1543) the final stanza reads "Les tiens enfans d'entre tes mains impures." The complete text of Macrin's version is printed on pp. 79-80.

6. In two successive books of the *Aeneid* Virgil employs the image of offspring torn from their mother which closes Macrin's translation. Its first appearance occurs when in the underworld Aeneas observes children snatched from their mothers by death: "quos dulcis vitae exsortis et ab ubere raptos" (6, 428); the second appearance of the image involves the portrait of a deer taken from its mother: "Tyrrhidae pueri quem matris ab ubere raptum" (7, 484).

7. Philippe Martinon, *Les Strophes* (Paris, 1912), p. 17.

8. See Laumonier's *Ronsard*, p. xlviii, n., for a justification of this interpretation in opposition to the Chamard thesis that Peletier was referring to subject matter.

9. Not all of Horace's *carmina* are stanzaic in nature. Those written in the Greater Asclepiad meter present a single series of verses of uniform length. In both the *Carminum libri quatuor* of 1530 and the *Odarum libri tres* of 1546 Macrin includes poems that are not written in stanzas. These facts may explain why one of the two psalms translated by Maurice Scève and published in 1542 is presented in decasyllabic couplets and why two of Du Bellay's odes (I and XII) among the *Vers lyriques* of 1549 are written in *rimes plates*.

10. See Claude Longeon, "Maurice Scève, traducteur des psaumes," in *Etudes seiziémistes offertes à Monsieur le Professeur V.-L. Saulnier* (Geneva, 1980), pp. 193-204.

11. The similarity between "A ceulx" and psalm 72 had already been noted by Juge, p. 377. The others I have cited are not mentioned by Juge, who does, however, catalogue two possible borrowings by Peletier from Marot's chansons (pp. 376-77).

12. The pertinent chapter of *Les Recherches* does, after all, introduce Bèze as "braue Poëte Latin & François" (p. 615). Should Bèze represent, to some degree, the neo-Latin movement of the day, we can better understand also why Pasquier's list of "auant-coureurs" does not single out, as Laumonier would have expected, a more distinguished neo-Latin poet, such as Jean Salmon Macrin.

13. See my " 'L'Adonis' de Ronsard et Andrea Navagero," *BHR*, 43 (1981), 155-58.

14. The influence of Amomo was proposed by Molinier in his general study of Saint-Gelais, p. 428. The two poets apparently knew each other. In his "Selva al christianissimo re di Francia, Francesco primo," Amomo writes: "Sangelesse gentil mi sappresenta / Che uerga i fogli d'amoroso inchiostro" (*Rime*, sig. G8^r). Pseudo-Theocritus provides, of course, the inspiration for vv. 113-20. From Virgil Saint-Gelais may have drawn the allusion of vv. 87-88; more certain echoes of Virgil are discussed on p. 77.

15. Virgil does no less in Book IV of the *Aeneid*, where a variation on the theme of IX, 224-25 describes Dido's agitated state.

Chapter IV

1. A particularly interesting example of this common appreciation for light verse is provided by Du Bellay himself. A volume published in 1560 contains his translation into Latin of "Du rousseau et de la rousse" (Blanchemain, I, 208-09), Saint-Gelais's recounting of the creation of the redhead, its consequences and the reasons why redheaded men and women never get along.

2. Vv. 6 and 7 of Blanchemain's edition read "Les rouges sont plaincte, en l'autre moitié, / Non point de vous, mais de Dieu sans pitié." The passage should read

"Les rouges font plaincte," as both MSS fr. 878 and 885 and the 1574 edition of Saint-Gelais's poetry indicate.

3. Witness, for example, the success of Carroset's *Blason des couleurs* and Rabelais's insistence on the young prince's colors in *Gargantua*, VIII.

4. For the text of this poem, see pp. 101-02.

5. For a discussion of the origin of this version of the dizain and of my reasons for quoting it, see pp. 108-09.

6. Guillaume Colletet, *Traité de l'épigramme*, ed. Pasquale A. Jannini (Geneva, 1965), p. 54. For further discussion of this point, see my "Saint-Gelais and the Epigrammatic Mode," to be published by French Forum Monographs with other papers presented at the March 1983 symposium on pre-Pléiade poetry held at the University of New Orleans. The volume will be edited by Jerry C. Nash.

7. Is there some relationship between this fact and the appearance of a second sonnet in *L'Olive* based on the same Italian source? If sonnet XLVII was intended to demonstrate a surer command of the material used in the poem just discussed, then Du Bellay certainly succeeded:

> Le doulx sommeil paix et plaisir m'ordonne,
> Et le reveil guerre et douleur m'aporte:
> Le faulx me plaist, le vray me deconforte:
> Le jour tout mal, la nuit tout bien me donne.
>
> S'il est ainsi, soit en toute personne
> La verité ensevelie et morte.
> O animaulx de plus heureuse sorte,
> Dont l'œil six mois le dormir n'abandonne!
>
> Que le sommeil à la mort soit semblant,
> Que le veiller de vie ait le semblant,
> Je ne le dy, et le croy' moins encores.
>
> Ou s'il est vray, puis que le jour me nuist
> Plus que la mort, ô mort, veilles donq' ores
> Clore mes yeulx d'une eternelle nuit.

Although the middle sections of the poem constitute a substantial development of the Italian themes, the source material dominates the first quatrain. But now the antitheses follow in a coherent fashion, and the development invented by Du Bellay follows upon the antitheses with an ease quite lacking in sonnet XXVIII.

8. See Grahame Castor, *Pléiade Poetics* (Cambridge, 1964), ch. 6, and Glyn P. Norton, "Translation Theory in Renaissance France: The Poetic Controversy," *Renaissance and Reformation*, 11 (1975), 30-44.

9. Read "reckoning." See Huguet, under "raconter" (1).

10. Since Saint-Gelais's poem appears in the 1547 edition of his works, it was readily available to Du Bellay.

11. Philip J. Ford, "George Buchanan's Court Poetry and the Pléiade," *French Studies*, 34 (1980), 137-52.

12. See below, p. 119, n. 4.

13. That is, "Laissez la verde couleur," "Ces six œillets," "Cent mille foys," "Si j'ay du bien," the adaptations from Claudian and Horace.

Chapter V

1. The song "Qui celera laffection" and its response "Quand vous verrez un serviteur," the eleventh and twelfth poems in the collection of 1545, appear much earlier in the *Oeuvres* of 1547.

2. The temptation did not pass with this work. Consider the *recueils* of songs printed c. 1550 and in 1555 (sigla D and F in the list of collated texts of "Laissez la verde couleur"). In addition to printing the pertinent songs by Saint-Gelais, the earlier collection reproduces six other songs from the Du Moulin anthology, and of those six, four are included in the collection of 1555 and printed in the same order.

3. The *Oeuvres* of 1547 offers yet another version of this dizain:

> Cent mille fois, & en cent mille sortes
> Ie baiseray ceste bouche, & ces yeulx
> Lors que mes mains plus que les tiennent [sic] fortes
> Te rendront prinse, & moy victorieux.
> Mais en baisant mon œil trop curieux
> De veoir le bien que la bouche luy cache
> Se tire arriere, & seul à iouir tasche
> De la beaulté qu'il pert quand on luy bousche [sic].
> Deuinez donc si vn autre me fasche
> Puis que mes yeulx sont ialoux de ma bouche?
>
> (pp. 35-36)

Of uneven value (the readings for vs. 8 seem particularly corrupt), the text does serve to point out again to what degree Blanchemain misleads us when he reproduces the title page of the 1547 edition and appears to do likewise for the text of the poems that follow. For the variants in vv. 2, 3, 4 and 6, we can only observe their existence and wish we knew more about the source of the poems printed in the *Oeuvres* of 1547.

4. For a carefully reasoned justification of the argument that Saint-Gelais imitated Wyatt and not Wyatt's source (a sonnet by Sannazaro), see John Berdan, "The Migration of a Sonnet," *MLN*, 23 (1908), 33-36. Wyatt's poem is quoted from Kenneth Muir's *Collected Poems of Sir Thomas Wyatt* (London, 1949), p. 25. The relationship between "Voyant ces monts" and Wyatt requires that we review the date of Chantilly MS 523. Noting that three poems by Saint-Gelais in the manuscript relate to Montmorency's appointment as Connétable (February 1538), but that there are no other poems "die uns veranlassten, die Anfertigung der Handschrift einer greifbar späteren Zeit zuzuweisen" (p. 44), Becker equates the preparation of the manuscript with Montmorency's elevation. Yet Wyatt's earliest visit to the French court occurred in December 1539. Unless Saint-Gelais somehow knew of Wyatt's sonnet prior to the poet's arrival at court, Chantilly MS 523 must have been prepared at a somewhat later time than Becker suggests.

5. Blanchemain gives "leur," adding, "Les Mss. m'ont fourni la leçon que je donne" (I, 79). If he is referring to a manuscript reading such as we find in Chantilly MS 523 ("Mille trouppeaux y prennent leur pasture"), then we discover further evidence of the unreliable nature of this edition, since Blanchemain will have conflated two quite different versions of the line.

6. On the date of the Chantilly MS, see n. 4 to this chapter. Since MS B.N. fr. 878 contains pièces de circonstance written for court festivities in 1548, 1554, 1556 and 1557, it must have been prepared well after the *Oeuvres* of 1547.

7. The dizain "Ha petit chien" appears in two different versions in Chantilly MS 523 (ff. 136^r and 185^v). Neither text corresponds exactly to the poem printed in the *Oeuvres* of 1547 (pp. 31-32) or to the work as published by Blanchemain (I, 97).

SELECT BIBLIOGRAPHY

Alamanni, Luigi. *Opere toscane*. Lyon, 1532.

Amomo. *Rime toscane*. Venice, 1538.

Becker, Philipp August. *Mellin de Saint-Gelais: Eine kritische Studie*. Vienna and Leipzig, 1924.

Bèze, Théodore de. *Les Juvenilia*. Ed. Alexandre Machard. Paris, 1879.

Bourbon, Nicolas. *Nugarum libri octo*. Lyon, 1538.

Cartier, Alfred, and Adolphe Chennevière. "Antoine du Moulin, Valet de Chambre de la Reine de Navarre." *RHLF*, 2 (1895), 469-91; 3 (1896), 90-106, 218-44.

Chamard, Henri. *Joachim Du Bellay*. Lille, 1900; rpt. Geneva, 1969.

Chansons nouvellement composées sur plusieurs chants, tant de musique que rustique. Paris, 1548.

Chardavoine, Jean. *Le Recueil des plus belles et excellentes chansons*. Paris, 1576.

Cotgrave, Randle. *A Dictionarie of the French and English Tongues*. London, 1611.

Des Périers, Bonaventure. *Recueil des oeuvres de feu Bonaventure des Périers*. Lyon, 1544.

Dottin, Georges. "Aspects littéraires de la chanson 'musicale' à l'époque de Marot." *RSH*, 116 (1964), 425-32.

Du Bellay, Joachim. *La Deffence et illustration de la langue francoyse*. Ed. Henri Chamard. Paris, 1966.

———. *Oeuvres poétiques*. Ed. Henri Chamard. 6 vols. Paris, 1908-1931.

Du Guillet, Pernette. *Rymes*. Ed. Victor E. Graham. Geneva, 1968.

Du Pont, Gracien. *Art et science de rhétorique métriffiée*. Toulouse, 1539.

Fabri, Pierre. *Le grant et vrai art de pleine rhétorique*. Ed. A. Héron. 3 vols. Rouen, 1889-1890.

Françon, Marcel. *Poèmes de transition (XVe-XVIe siècles), rondeaux du ms. 402 de Lille*. Cambridge, Mass., 1938.

Guy, Henry. *Histoire de la poésie française au XVIe siècle*. 2 vols. Paris, 1926.

Hutton, James. *The Greek Anthology in France*. Ithaca, N.Y., 1946; rpt. New York, 1967.

Jasinski, Max. *Histoire du sonnet en France*. Douai, 1903; rpt. Geneva, 1970.

Jeffery, Brian, ed. *Chanson Verse of the Early Renaissance*. 2 vols. London, 1971-1976.

Jourda, Pierre. "Sur quelques poésies faussement attribuées à Saint-Gelais." *RHLF*, 31 (1924), 303-05.

Juge, Clément. *Jacques Peletier du Mans (1517-1582)*. Paris, 1907.

Laumonier, Paul. *Commentaire*. See Séché, Léon.

———. *Ronsard, poète lyrique*. 2nd ed. Paris, 1923.

Legrand, Philippe Ernest, ed. and trans. *Bucoliques grecs*. Paris, 1967. [Contains texts of Theocritus, Pseudo-Theocritus and Bion.]

Lesure, François. *Musicians and Poets of the French Renaissance*. New York, 1955.

Marguerite de Navarre. *Chansons spirituelles*. Ed. Georges Dottin. Geneva, 1971.

Marot, Clément. *Oeuvres*. Ed. Claude Albert Mayer. 5 vols. London, 1958-1970.

———. *Les Psaumes de Clément Marot*. Ed. Samuel J. Lenselink. Assen, 1969.

McFarlane, Ian D. "Poésie néo-latine et poésie de langue vulgaire à l'époque de la Pléiade." In *Acta Conventus neo-latini lovaniensis*. Eds. Jozef IJsewijn and Eckhardt Kessler. Munich, 1973, pp. 389-403.

McKenzie, Kenneth. *Concordanza delle Rime di Francesco Petrarca*. New Haven, Conn., 1912.

Molinier, Henri-Joseph. *Mellin de Saint-Gelays (1490?-1558)*. Paris, 1910; rpt. Geneva, 1968.

Pasquier, Etienne. *Les Recherches de la France*. Paris, 1621.

Peletier du Mans, Jacques. *L'Art poétique*. Ed. André Boulanger. Paris, 1930.

———, trans. *L'Art poétique d'Horace*. Paris, 1545.

———. *Les Oeuvres poétiques*. Paris, 1547.

———. *Les Oeuvres poétiques*. Ed. Marcel Françon. Rochecorbon, 1958.

Plattard, Jean. Review of *Mellin de Saint-Gelais: Eine kritische Studie*, by P.A. Becker. *RSS*, 12 (1925), 182-86.

Ronsard, Pierre de. *Oeuvres complètes*. Ed. Paul Laumonier. 20 vols. Paris, 1914-1975.

Saint-Gelais, Mellin de. *Oeuvres complètes*. Ed. Prosper Blanchemain. 3 vols. Paris, 1873.

Salmon Macrin, Jean. *Carminum libri quatuor*. Paris, 1530.

———. *Naeniarum libri tres*. Paris, 1550.

———. *Odarum libri tres*. Paris, 1546.

Saulnier, Verdun-Louis. "Etude sur Pernette du Guillet et ses *Rymes*." *BHR*, 4 (1944), 7-119.

———. "Mellin de Saint-Gelais, Pernette du Guillet et l'air 'Conde Claros.'" *BHR*, 32 (1970), 525-32.

———. "Remarques sur la tradition des textes de Mellin de Saint-Gelais." *Bulletin de l'Association Guillaume Budé* (June 1953), pp. 13-19.

Sébillet, Thomas. *Art poétique françoys*. Ed. Félix Gaiffe. Paris, 1910.

Second, Jean. *Basia*. Lyon, 1539.

Séché, Léon, ed. *Oeuvres poétiques de Jacques Peletier du Mans, avec une Notice biographique, un Commentaire et des Notes par Paul Laumonier*. Paris, 1904.

Smith, Pauline M., and Claude Albert Mayer. "La Première Epigramme française: Clément Marot, Jean Boucher et Michel d'Amboise. Définition, sources, antériorité." *BHR*, 32 (1970), 579-602.

Thibault, Geneviève. "Musique et poésie en France au XVIe siècle avant les 'Amours' de Ronsard." In *Musique et poésie au XVIe siècle*. Paris, 1954, pp. 79-88.

Tilley, Arthur. "From Marot to Ronsard." In *Mélanges de littérature, d'histoire et de philologie offerts à Paul Laumonier*. Paris, 1935, pp. 131-61.

Vianey, Joseph. *Le Pétrarquisme en France au XVIe siècle*. Paris, 1909.

Wilkins, Nigel, ed. *One Hundred Ballades, Rondeaux and Virelais from the Late Middle Ages*. Cambridge, 1969.

INDEX

FRENCH FORUM MONOGRAPHS

.

27. Donald M. Frame and Mary B. McKinley, eds. *Columbia Montaigne Conference Papers*. 1981.
28. Jean-Pierre Dens. *L'Honnête Homme et la critique du goût: Esthétique et société au XVIIe siècle*. 1981.
29. Vivian Kogan. *The Flowers of Fiction: Time and Space in Raymond Queneau's Les Fleurs bleues*. 1982.
30. Michael Issacharoff et Jean-Claude Vilquin, éds. *Sartre et la mise en signe*. 1982.
31. James W. Mileham. *The Conspiracy Novel: Structure and Metaphor in Balzac's Comédie humaine*. 1982.
32. Andrew G. Suozzo, Jr. *The Comic Novels of Charles Sorel: A Study of Structure, Characterization and Disguise*. 1982.
33. Margaret Whitford. *Merleau-Ponty's Critique of Sartre's Philosophy*. 1982.
34. Gérard Defaux. *Le Curieux, le glorieux et la sagesse du monde dans la première moitié du XVIe siècle: L'exemple de Panurge (Ulysse, Démosthène, Empédocle)*. 1982.
35. Doranne Fenoaltea. *"Si haulte Architecture." The Design of Scève's* Délie. 1982.
36. Peter Bayley and Dorothy Gabe Coleman, eds. *The Equilibrium of Wit: Essays for Odette de Mourgues*. 1982.
37. Carol J. Murphy. *Alienation and Absence in the Novels of Marguerite Duras*. 1982.
38. Mary Ellen Birkett. *Lamartine and the Poetics of Landscape*. 1982.
39. Jules Brody. *Lectures de Montaigne*. 1982.
40. John D. Lyons. *The Listening Voice: An Essay on the Rhetoric of Saint-Amant*. 1982.
41. Edward C. Knox. *Patterns of Person: Studies in Style and Form from Corneille to Laclos*. 1983.
42. Marshall C. Olds. *Desire Seeking Expression: Mallarmé's "Prose pour des Esseintes."* 1983.
43. Ceri Crossley. *Edgar Quinet (1803-1875): A Study in Romantic Thought*. 1983.
44. Rupert T. Pickens, ed. *The Sower and His Seed: Essays on Chrétien de Troyes*. 1983.
45. Barbara C. Bowen. *Words and the Man in French Renaissance Literature*. 1983.
46. Clifton Cherpack. *Logos in Mythos. Ideas and Early French Narrative*. 1983.
47. Donald Stone, Jr. *Mellin de Saint-Gelais and Literary History*. 1983

French Forum, Publishers, Inc.
P.O. Box 5108, Lexington, Kentucky 40505

Publishers of *French Forum*, a journal of literary criticism

Frances Fyfield is a criminal law̸̸̸̸̸̸̸̸ ion that has
inspired and info ned her novels though not exclusively.
She is widely translated, and a winner of the Crime Writers'
Association Silver Dagger Award and of the Grand Prix de
Littérature Policière in France. Several of her books have
been televised. She lives in London and in Deal.

'Thank God for Frances, she reminds us that horror lurks
beneath the surface of the most humdrum lives, and that
criminals are also human beings . . . The Queen of the
Psychological Thriller. If you haven't tried her, start with this
novel . . . You will soon become addicted' A. N. Wilson

'[She] has an intense human compassion, a great gift as a
novelist, and a capacity, like her characters, for having a
good time, and giving the reader the same' Fay Weldon

'[She] writes with impressive empathy . . . there is a vein of
humour, too, in this fine book, which is as taut and sus-
penseful as the very best of thrillers' *Telegraph*

'[She] is fearless in her portrayal of Isabel's suppressed rage
and suffocating guilt, while Serena, flickering in and out of
self-awareness like a broken strip-light, is a genuinely tragic
creation' *Independent on Sunday*

'Compelling' *Daily Mail*